SCANDINAVIAN BRITAIN

SCANDINAVIAN
BRITAIN

by
W. G. COLLINGWOOD, M.A., F.S.A.

PROFESSOR OF FINE ART, UNIVERSITY COLLEGE,
READING. EDITOR TO THE CUMBERLAND AND
WESTMORLAND ANTIQUARIAN AND
ARCHAEOLOGICAL SOCIETY

First published in 1908

Facsimile reprint 1993
by Llanerch Publishers, Felinfach
ISBN 1897853211

Shetland

Papa Stour
Foula

Petlar
Whalsay
Bressay

Fair I^d

Papa Westray
Rousay
Maeshow
Hoy

N. Ronaldsay
Sanday
Stronsay
Kirkwall
Margaret's Hope
S. Ronaldsay

Orkney

Dingwall

Mar

Dunnottar

Kirriemuir

Strathearn
Scone
St. Andrews

Stirling
Dumbarton

Lothian
Strathclyde

BERNICIA

Galloway

Solway

Whithorn

Lindisfarne
Bamborough

Duncansby Head
Wick
Caithness

Isle Man
Peel
Maughold

Gosforth

Tynemouth
Jarrow Wearmouth
Chester le Street
Durham

Whitby
Cleveland

SCANDINAVIAN BRITAIN

Scale of Statute Miles
0 10 20 30 40 50   100

The Danelaw ————
Norse Settlements ————

Crangford
Lough

Lambey
Howth

Wicklow

Anglesey

Ormeshead

Bardsey

Amounderness

Ripon

York
Riccall
Leeds

B R A
N E D

Stamford
bridge
Beverley
Holderness

R. Humber

Grantham
Driesey
Lincoln

Lindsey

Chester

Bakewell

Derby
Nottingham

The Five

St. Davids
Milford

Ceredigion

Welshpool

Shrewsbury

Repton
Stafford

Bridgnorth

R. Wye
R. Usk
Hereford

Rugby
Warwick
Worcester

Morganwg

Llanwit
Swansea
S.W. Holms

Gloucester

Boroughs
Leicester Stamford Crowland
Peterborough
Huntingdon
Northampton
Bedford
Cambridge

Norwich

Thetford
St. Edmunds

E A S T
A N G L I A

Colchester
Hertford
Maldon
ESSEX
Mersea I^d

Lundy

Athelney

Bristol
Chippenham

Abingdon
Dorchester
Wallingford

Oxford

London

Reading

Rochester
Milton

Sheppey
Thanet
Canterbury
Dover

Wilton
Salisbury

Winchester

S E X

Appledore

Hastings

Exeter
Kingsbridge

Bridport

Dorchester
Wareham
Portland
Swanage

I.of
Wight

Chichester

Etaples

SCANDINAVIAN
BRITAIN

CONTENTS

PREFATORY NOTE

IN the part of this work for which I am responsible, that is to say from page 43 onward, kind assistance in proof-reading has been given by the Rev. Edmund McClure, Secretary to the S.P.C.K., and by Mr. Albany F. Major, Editor to the Viking Club. The chapters on Northumbria (pp. 119–181) have been read by Mr. William Brown, F.S.A., and the chapter on Orkney by Mr. Alfred W. Johnston, F.S.A. Scot., Editor of *Orkney and Shetland Old Lore*.

W. G. C.

SCANDINAVIAN BRITAIN

I. THE EARLIEST RAIDS

"Whilst the pious King Bertric was reigning over the western parts of the English, and the innocent people, spread through their plains, were enjoying themselves in tranquillity and yoking their oxen to the plough, suddenly there arrived on the coast a fleet of Danes, not large, but of three ships only: this was their first arrival. When this became known, the king's officer, who was already dwelling in the town of Dorchester, leaped on his horse and rode with a few men to the port, thinking that they were merchants and not enemies. Giving his commands as one that had authority, he ordered them to be sent to the king's town; but they slew him on the spot, and all who were with him. The name of this officer was Beaduheard. A.D. 787. And the number of years was above 344 from the time when Hengist and Horsa arrived in Britain."

Such was the tradition, a century and a half later, of the beginning of Scandinavian Britain. Æthelwerd, ealdorman and historian, who wrote the notice, had access to special sources of information, such as the royal family to which he belonged must have preserved; and his story tallies with the shorter entry of the

43

Chronicle that "three ships of Northmen [MS. A, 'of Danes'] came from Hærethaland ; and then the reeve rode to the place, and would have driven them to the king's town, because he knew not who they were ; and there they slew him."

If there is any discrepancy between the two tales, Æthelwerd's has the advantage. For a century after this date the word "Northmen" is not used of the Vikings in the English chronicles. The entry is an interpolation, about which it is hardly worth inquiring too minutely. The date, usually given with definiteness if not with accuracy in the Chronicle, is wanting ; we are only told that it was in the reign of King Beorhtric. The place is not named, whereas the annals are otherwise careful to name the sites of battles, though we cannot always identify them. The three ships are suspiciously like the three keels of Hengist and Horsa, to whom Æthelwerd actually refers ; he also giving for date only the marriage of Beorhtric, in whose days the event happened. There must have been some song or story of a raid, which an editor of chronicles has tried to turn into history. The word "Hærethaland" does not appear in the Chron. MS. A, and is a later insertion into an entry which itself is an interpolation. Consequently, it is useless to build a theory of the home of these first Vikings—to hold, with Munch, that they came from Hardeland in Jutland, or, with others, that Hordaland, the country of the Hardanger fjord in Norway, is meant.

This is not the only instance of doubtful or fallacious statement in the history of the Vikings in Britain, as we find it in old writings and in modern authors. Any account of the period must be tentative and provisional, depending on annals and sagas which cannot be trusted implicitly, and on inferences which a wider knowledge may upset. But there is one class of misstatements which ought to be cleared away at the beginning—the wide-spread belief in the pre-historic Viking. There is no reason to assert that Scandinavian sea-robbers, as distinct from the Angles and Saxons of the fifth and sixth centuries, appeared on the coasts of Britain before the end of the eighth century.

In a well-known book, justly popular on account of its wealth of illustration, the late Paul du Chaillu used the argument from this doubtful entry of " Northmen from Hærethaland " to enforce his idea that the " so-called Saxons," as he was careful to call them, were precisely the same people as the Scandinavian Vikings, whose sagas, he remarked, never called the English " Saxons," as the Celtic nations did. He contended that from Roman days to the twelfth century there was a continuous stream of invasion setting in from the Baltic shores to Britain ; *littus Saxonicum* was a Viking settlement ; the English came from Engelholm on the Cattegat, and from places named Engeln in Sweden ; Tacitus mentioned the boats of the Suiones, and surely their " mighty fleets " must have been employed between the days of Agricola and those of Charlemagne in more than local traffic ; the whole millennium was a Viking Age.

Burton also (*Hist. Scotland*, i. 302) wrote that

"droves of them (Scando-Gothic sea-rovers) came over centuries before the Hengest and Horsa of the stories, if they were not indeed the actual large-boned, red-haired men whom Agricola described to his son-in-law." He supported his theory with a reference to Dr. Collingwood Bruce, the historian of the Roman Wall, who, describing an altar found near Thirlwall about 1757, said: "Hodgson (the historian of Northumberland) remarks that *Vithris* was a name of Odin, as we find in the Death-song of Lodbroc . . If *Veteres* and the Scandinavian Odin are identical, we are thus furnished with evidence of the early settlement of the Teutonic tribes in England." But this altar, and another he mentions from Condercum (Benwell Hill, Northumberland.), compared with altars now at Chesters on the Wall, and inscribed "Dibus Veteribus," are more likely to have been dedicated "To the Ancient Gods" than to the *Vidhrir* of the Edda, many hundred years later. Huxley (in Laing's *Prehistoric Remains of Caithness*) suggested that by anthropological evidence, long before the well-known Norse and Danish invasions, a stream of Scandinavians had come into Scotland; Professor Rolleston connected the Round-headed men of the Bronze Age in York-shire with Denmark, but this refers to the racial origin of tribes three thousand years ago. Such facts do not support speculation, misled by the hope of finding grains of truth in Ossianic poetry, Arthurian legend and late Scandinavian sagas, in all of which there is the same tendency to antedate incidents and to lose the perspective of history.

The Ossianic poems are full of references to Lochlann and the Norse as the opponents of Fionn mac Cumhall, whom Macpherson curiously called " Fingal," which means " the Norseman," and as a personal name was introduced and used by the Vikings.   Irish and Hebridean folklore relates that before the Christian era the islands were ruled by sea-kings called Fomorians (from *fomhor*, a giant, a pirate), and popularly identified with the Scandinavian pirates. The confusion existed in old Irish historians; Duald Mac Firbis, writing in the seventeenth century and following authors of the fourteenth and fifteenth centuries, in his tract on the Fomorians and the Lochlannachs (edited by Prof. Alex. Bugge, Christiania, 1905) classed them together, though he knew that " the Fomorians were the first who waged war against the country " of Ireland.   " The Wars of the Gaedhil and the Gaill " tells an impossible tale of the mythological King Nuada of the Silver Hand and the Fomorians who came from Lochlann or Norway : and when the Norse King Magnus Barefoot of the eleventh century became an important figure in Celtic folklore, as he was in the sixteenth century, the story-tellers found no difficulty in pitting him against Fionn mac Cumhall in a great battle fought on the island of Arran.   Giraldus Cambrensis tells the tale of Gurmundus, who, though a Norwegian, came from Africa in the sixth century to Ireland, and then invading Britain, took Cirencester from its Welsh king, and ruled the realm.   Now late chronicles, like the *Book of Hyde* and *Gaimar*, called

Guthorm-Æthelstan "Gurmund"; he held Cirencester in 879-880. Here again we have no trace of a pre-historic Viking, but only of history distorted and antedated. The grains of truth in all these Celtic legends must be looked for in the real events of the ninth to the twelfth centuries.

Not only in folklore, but in well-meant historical study the same tendency is visible. In the *Annals of the Four Masters* under A.D. 743 occurs this entry: "Arasgach, abbot of Muicinsi Reguil, was drowned." A similar entry appears in the Ulster *Annals* for 747; meaning that the abbot of the "Hog-island of St. Regulus" (Muckinish in Lough Derg) so met his death. But according to John O'Donovan's note (ed. 1849) the former editor, Dr. O'Conor, had read for "Reguil," "re gallaibh,"—the abbot of Muckinish was drowned "by strangers," the Gaill or Vikings, half a century before they were otherwise heard of. Following this error, Moore in his history described an attack on "Rechrain," meaning Lambey, and the drowning of the abbot's pigs by the Danes. "Thus," says O'Donovan, "has Irish history been manufactured."

Thus, too, English history. Gaimar, to whom we are often indebted for a bright touch on our early annals, places the story of Havelock the Dane in the days of Constantine, successor to King Arthur. Now Havelock is the Cumbrian legendary form of Olaf Cuaran, the tenth century king of York and Dublin (see pp. 138, 139), and though the story is woven from early traditions, the setting is antedated. Many of the incidents worked into the Arthurian cycle may date from the times of Ælfred and Eadmund Ironside, whose series of battles with Halfdan and Knut offers analogies to Arthur's fights with the heathen. The Arthurian legend took form in the Viking Age, and was put back into the "good old times" according to the use and wont of story-tellers, but contains some Scandinavian elements. For instance, the horse of Sir Gawain, according to Prof. Gollancz, has been evolved out of the boat of Wade, the hero of the Völund myth ; *Tristram and Isolt* (a Pictish and a Teutonic name) seems to be a love-story from Strathclyde not earlier than the tenth or the eleventh century. That there are quite ancient Celtic myths in the Arthurian cycle is not disputed, but much of the material, as in the Ossianic le-gends, comes from that stirring and fruitful age of storm and stress when the contact of many various races and cultures, especially in the north of Britain, produced a really romantic era.

Thus, again, has Scandinavian history been manu-factured. The Ynglinga saga (chap. xlv.) tells how Ivar Widefathom, who must have "flourished" in the seventh century, subdued the fifth part of Eng-land. For Ivar Widefathom read Ivar "the Bone-less" of two hundred years later, and we come nearer to historical truth, for "Northumbria is the fifth part of England," as Egil's saga says ; and this later Ivar, though himself not entirely free from legend-ary attributions, seems to have been the leading spirit of the conquest (p. 86). At the battle of Brávöll,

D

supposed to have been fought about 700 A.D., King
Harald Hilditönn is said (in *Sögubrot*) to have had
the help of Brat the Irishman and Orm the English.
There is no great absurdity in supposing that a stray
Westerner may have wandered into his service, but
when the *Fornmanna-sögur* tell us that he died at the
age of one hundred and eighty winters after owning a
kingdom in England, and this in the lifetime of Bede,
the mythical nature of the story is apparent.   Sigurd
Hring, his kinsman and opponent at Brávöll, "be-
thought him of the kingdom which Harald had
owned in England, and, before him, Ivar Widefathom,
then ruled by Ingjald, brother of Petr, Saxon king,"
or rather (not to make the story more absurd than it
need be) the " West Saxon king," for the þ, or Anglo-
Saxon *w*, has been misread.   So Sigurd invaded
Northumbria, fought battles in which Ingjald and his
son Ubbi fell, won the realm and left it under a
tributary King Olaf, son of Kinrik, cousin of Ivar
Widefathom, who was ultimately driven out by Eava,
son of Ubbi (Eoppa).   Munch (*Norske Folks Historie*, I., i., p. 281) points out that there were real Saxon
kings to tally with the story ; Ingild, brother of Ini of
Wessex, died 718 : but the whole account seems to
be a garbled version of affairs in the middle of the
tenth century, when Eirík (sometimes called Hiring,
or Hring) and Olaf Cuaran were disputing the kingdom of Northumbria.

Coming down to the threshold of history we have
the romantic figure of Ragnar Lodbrok, dragon-slayer,
and son-in-law of the great dragon-slayer Sigurd Faf-

nisbani. He, it is said, to outdo Hengist and Horsa and the Northmen from Hærethaland, set out to conquer England with *two* ships. Captured by Ælla of Northumberland, he was thrown into the pit of snakes. His sons, Ivar the Boneless and his brethren, avenged him by the great invasion and conquest; but their saga embroiders the true story with picturesque and mythical ornament. It tells how Ivar the Crafty, hanging back from the first fruitless attempt, bargained with Ælla for as much land as an ox-hide would cover,—the old Hengist and Horsa plot. Thus founding London (or York), he gained Ælla's confidence, brought his brothers' army back, and avenged his father with the torture of Ælla and St. Eadmund. The episode is not made more historical by placing the scene in Ireland, as Haliday (*Scandinavian Dublin*, p. 28) tries to do. A historic Ragnar was present at the siege of Paris in 845, and Ivar with his brethren conquered East Anglia and Northumbria; but the legendary part of the saga is merely one variant of the inevitable myth of explanation, invented to show why the Vikings attacked Britain, other variants being Roger of Wendover's tale of Berne the huntsman and Lothbrok, and Gaimar's of Buern Buzecarle.

It must be evident that such legends of prehistoric Vikings—Celtic, English and Scandinavian—are the natural growth of the story-telling genius at an age when the great movement was past. After every war we have a crop of novels about it. At the same time, the fact of piracy was no invention of the

Scandinavians. Thucydides has described exactly
the same circumstances in the Ægean at the dawn of
Greek history. Carausius in the third century of our
era was a sea-rover. St. Patrick was carried from
Britain by pirates of the fourth century, and escaped
from Ireland to Gaul in a merchant-ship. The life of
St. Columba is full of sea-faring; the "Celtic horror
of the sea" did not exist in the fifth century, when
the monks travelled far in their skin-boats and sailors
from Gaul visited Iona, when Erc stole the seals in
the monastery's preserves, and Joan mac Conal played
the pirate among the Hebrides, as Adamnan relates
(*Life of Columba*, i. 28, 41; ii. 41). These early
notices of piracy among Celts, with the fact that one
monastery fought another and that Irish kings attacked churches and slew monks, regardless of religious awe, surely explain the massacre of Eigg
(A.D. 617), in which Prof. A. Bugge sees a proof of
Scandinavian presence at a very early date (*Vikingerne*
i. p. 137). The two stories of this event—one, that
the monks trespassed on the pastures of the queen of
the country and suffered in consequence; and the
other, that pirates of the sea came and slew them—
are ingeniously reconciled by Skene (*Celtic Scotland*
ii. 153), but neither account requires the appearance
of Norse or Danish vikings. There was continual
sea-faring and piracy among the natives and more
immediate neighbours of our sea-coasts. St. Columban, in the sixth century, was sent in a merchant ship
from Nantes to Ireland, and Bishop Arculf in the
seventh century went from France to Iona on board a

trading-ship. In 684 Ecgfrith of Northumbria sent his army, under Berhtred, to Ireland, and ravaged Magh-breg, and in 685 Adamnan sailed to England to buy back the captives. In 728 the *Four Masters* mention a " marine fleet " of Dalriada which attacked Inisowen in Ulster. The English and Irish were already showing the example of the very deeds they lamented with such bitterness a little later. Is it to be supposed that no word of such events reached Scandinavia, when the chief sea-traders of the age were the Frisians, near neighbours of Denmark ? Why, one may ask, did not the Viking raids begin sooner ?

As a matter of fact, they did ; but we have no record stating that they reached Britain. About 515 King Chochilaicus, as Gregory of Tours calls him, or Hugleik, led a fleet from the Baltic to the mouth of the Meuse or the Rhine, and was overcome and slain by Theodebert, son of the Frankish king Theodoric. This is *Beowulf's* Hygelác, king of Goths ; and the existence of *Beowulf* shows that there was early connection, other than hostile, between Scandinavia and England. But the invasion of Hugleik, like the Anglo-Saxon settlement, was a part of the great " folk-wandering " movement, not a Viking raid of a few pirates adventuring for slaves and gold. Professor Alexander Bugge, in his recent works *Vikingerne,* i., 1904, and *Vesterlandenes Inflydelse paa Nordboernes i Vikingetiden,* 1905, points out that the period of Hugleik was full of such enterprises. Fifty years later (565) the Danes made a

similar expedition to the western seas from their
headquarters in Sjæland at Leira, where was the
royal hall, named, from the antlers of deer at its
gables, *Heorot*, or Hart. Here King Hrodgar (Roar),
son of Halfdan, and his nephew Hrolf Kraki, the
Skjöldungs, fought the Hadobards from the East
and drove them away; but in the end misfortune
came to the burg of the Skjöldungs, and Hrolf fell
with his men. Danes and Swedes in the folk-
wandering epoch were already conscious of some
collective nationality; race-union was begun; while
the inhabitants of Norway were scattered into separate
tribes and petty kingdoms until the beginning of
the true Viking age. The first steps to extension
of power westward must naturally have been taken
rom Denmark as a centre, the Swedes pushing east
to Russia. But Professor A. Bugge also thinks,
agreeing with H. Zimmer, that the Norse of Norway
had found their way across the sea to the Orkneys and
Shetland a hundred years before the Viking attacks are
recorded in England and Ireland. There seems to
be no reason to doubt that they did adventure on the
high seas somewhat sooner than the usually assigned
date; for Dicuil, writing about 825, describes islands
divided by narrow channels and swarming with sheep,
which seem to be the Færoes (sheep-isles), as inhabited a century before by Irish monks, but then
deserted on account of heathen pirates; and, in fact,
the colony of Grím Kamban was made in 825. But
by then the Viking Age had begun; and Prof. A.
Bugge would put their advent in Britain much earlier.

His views (*Vikingerne*, i. p. 134) may be summarised
thus :—

Long before Ireland was attacked, viz. A.D. 700 or
earlier, men from south-western Norway—Hordaland,
Ryfylke, Jæderen, and neighbouring settlements,—
may have sailed over the North Sea and landed in
Orkney and Shetland. Several Shetland place-names
are formed in a way which had gone out of fashion
when Iceland was colonised, as Dr. Jakob Jakobsen
notes (in *Aarböger for nordisk Oldkyndighed*, 1902).
Further, the Viking Age settlers had owned their land
so long that they could call it their *odal* or *udal*, and
the tradition was that jarl Torf-Einar took the odal
lands away from the bœndr, who got them back from
Sigurd Hlödver's son ; whereas in Iceland, colonised
late in the ninth century, no such word as *odal* is
used : the Icelanders who left their native country
under compulsion had their odals in Norway, not
in Iceland. With the Norse may have come Got-
landers ; stones inscribed with the earlier runes (of
the kind used before the Viking Age) and found in
Norway bear witness to a connexion with east Sweden
and Gotland, and in Gotland there is a series of
pillar-stones dating from 700 or earlier, with spirals
and other ornaments of a Celtic type, which suggests
intercourse between Celtic countries and the Baltic,
possibly by way of Orkney and Norway.

With regard to these three lines of argument it
might be answered that a connexion between Britain
and the Baltic in early ages need not be doubted, but
that it was more likely to have been by way of Frisia ;

and that there has been a tendency to antedate the development of Irish decorative art—Prof. A. Bugge elsewhere gives a seventh-century date to the Book of Kells—and consequently to antedate the monuments supposed to have been influenced from Ireland. The date of Torf-Einar's seizure of the odals cannot be much before the end of the ninth century, which would allow for two or three generations of settlers in Orkney after the period at which Dicuil indicates their arrival. And as Iceland was not colonised until 874, the earlier years of the ninth century are far enough back to explain archaic place-names in Shetland. Beyond that epoch there seems no need to go.

The true Viking Age began during the last years of the eighth century; and it began with raids on the coast nearest to Denmark. Lappenberg, in his *History of England under the Anglo-Saxon Kings* (Thorpe's tr., ii. p. 19), quotes an epistle of Bregowine to Lullus (who died in 786) mentioning " frequent attacks of wicked men on the provinces of the English or on the regions of Gaul." It is not clear that he meant Scandinavian pirates, but we are coming very near to the time and place where the earliest recorded attacks did occur; and when they once began they came thick and fast. However untrustworthy any given entry may be, Irish, English, and Frankish annals unite in asserting that Viking raids, outside the Baltic, began soon after this date, and continued from that time forward. Within the Baltic the Scandinavian tribes had been preying upon each other for centuries: now at last they found new worlds to conquer. It was not that they had never heard of Gaul and Britain, but that they had not been induced or emboldened to venture so far in small parties for the sake of robbery under arms.

What, then, was the reason, or occasion, of this sudden outburst? Steenstrup thought that overpopulation, through polygamy, had made emigration necessary: but the earlier raids were not emigration; and K. Maurer argued that Harald Fairhair's attempts to check emigration showed that Norway was not too crowded. J. R. Green, in his *Conquest of England*, suggested that as the unification of the small Scandinavian kingdoms had already begun, the more independent spirits preferred adventure and exile to alien rule; adding that it is needless to look further for a reason than the hope of plunder. But attempts at unification had begun long before this period in Denmark and Sweden, and in Norway Harald Fairhair's domination came after the Viking Age had already set in. The hope of plunder was no doubt the motive, but why should this date stand as the moment when such hopes were formed? Others have supposed that heathendom was making reprisals for Charlemagne's war on the Saxons; but this idea involves a solidarity among the Scandinavians, and a sentiment of religion, wholly foreign to all we know of them. The Viking raids may have been prompted partly by hate of the Christian invader, but they were not analogous to the Crusades; they simply meant that the people of the Baltic awoke to the possibility of successful

plundering on French, British, and Irish coasts—
places which, at an earlier date, they had not ventured
to assail.

The Saxon war, begun in 772 (Eginhard), brought
the people of Denmark directly into touch with
Western Europe. Sigfred, the Danish king, received
Widukind, the Saxon chief, when he sought refuge
from Charlemagne's armies. In 777 an embassy was
sent from Sigfred to Charlemagne, and though the
Danes took no general part in the struggle, in 803
Godfred, the successor of Sigfred, advanced with a
fleet to Sleswick to protect his land, and in 808, after
a raid across the Elbe, he built the first Danework
in the hope of making invasion impossible. This
earliest earthwork has been described by Mr. H.
A. Kjær in *The Saga-book of the Viking Club* (iv.
pp. 313–325). The conduct of the war must have
opened the eyes of the Baltic folk to the opportunity
of plundering in regions which, up to that time, they
had regarded as beyond them in every sense. They
found that monasteries were wealthy and unprotected ;
gold and silver, rich clothes, wine and dainties, cattle
and captives to sell in the market, could be had for the
taking, in places which they had thought unassail-
able and impracticable. When once this new world
was opened up, as in later ages America was opened,
adventure was the obvious duty of every one who
wished to better himself. But as we now-a-days find
that a war teaches us geography, so it needed the
Saxon war to call attention to the wealth and weakness
of these western regions.

About this time the overking of Denmark ruled
also Vestfold, the west coast of the Vík, now the
fjord of Christiania in Norway; there was hardly anything in the nature of a political distinction between
the people on the opposite coasts of the Skagerrack;
the language was much the same, and the ethnological
differences noticed later as distinguishing Black-pirates,
or Danes, from White-pirates, or Norse, in Ireland
cannot have been important in the case of sea-farers
united rather than divided by the narrow seas. The
mountains of Norway, cutting up the country into
deep valleys, were a more effectual bar to intercourse,
and the true Norse were those of the Bergen and
Trondhjem fjords and Gudbrandsdal. From the beginning the English regarded the invaders as Danes;
the word "Northmen" was the French name. To
the Franks all the invaders came from the North,
and the name did not mean people of Norway, which
indeed Prof. Noreen derives—as Munch (*Norske Folks
Historie*, I. i. 67) hinted—not from "north," but from
nór, a sea-loch. The Northmen of Normandy were
mostly of Danish origin—that is to say, from the
country later known as Denmark. Irish annals called
the invaders the Gaill (foreigners) or Gentiles, or
heathen, until 836, when the *Four Masters* chronicle
the arrival of sixty ships of *Northmen*, and, in 841,
three fleets *Normannorum*—a Latin word in the
Gaelic text. In 846 the same annals mention *Tomh-
rair erla tanaisi righ Lochlainne*, jarl Thórir, tanist
(heir) of the King of Lochlann. Then, in 847, "a
fleet of seven score ships of the people of the king

of the foreigners came to contend with the foreigners
that were in Ireland before them;" and, in 850,
"the Dubhgoill arrived in Athcliath (Dublin) and
slaughtered the Finghoill." The Ulster Annals name
the Lochlanns in 839, and the Black and White
Gaill in 847. Now Duald Mac Firbis says, "The
writings of the Irish call a Lochlannaigh by the
name Goill : they also call some of them Dubhlochlannaigh, *i. e.* black Gentiles, which was applied to
the Danes of Dania, *i.e.* Denmark: Finn-Lochlannaigh,
i. e. fair Gentiles, *i. e.* the people of Ioruaighe, *i. e.* the
people of Norwegia :" and Keating explained Loch-
lonnaigh (*sic*) as "powerful on lakes or on the sea,"
from *lonn*, strong ; and gave the name to the Danes
(quoted in O'Donovan's *Four Masters*, p. 616). Still
the name of Lochlann seems to have been used as a
geographical expression ; but if it means " the country
of lochs," early Irish geography may have applied
it to Denmark, where the Limafjord and the Belts
are land-locked waters, as characteristic as the fjords
of Norway. If Duald Mac Firbis is right, the word
Dubhlochlannaigh shows that there was no distinction
at first in the minds of the Irish between Norway
and Denmark. *Fuarlochlann*, the cold Lochlann, is
used by him, perhaps for Norway. Prof. S. Bugge,
however, finds in the name *Onphile jarla* (*Wars of
the Gaedhil*, 845 A.D.) "Án Fila-jarl," earl of the
Fjala-folk (north of Sogne-fjord) in Norway ; which, if
established, is remarkable (see A. Bugge's *Vesterlandenes Indfl.*, p. 108).

The name Viking (wicing) is used once in English

chronicles (*A.-Sax. Chron.* under 982). It is found in the
Epinal Glossary, and therefore was known long before
the Scandinavian invasions (W. H. Stevenson, *Eng.
Hist. Rev.* xix., p. 143). Dr. Lawrence has suggested
that it comes from the Anglo-Saxon *wigan, wigian*, to
fight, from which the usual substantive is *wiggend* or
wigend, a warrior. *Liðvícingas* occurs in "*Widsith*,"
corresponding to the Icelandic *Liðungar*, the men from
Lid in the Vík of Norway, though the reading of one
MS. in the chronicles (A.D. 885) of *Lidwicingas* for
Lidwiccas suggests that Bretons might be meant in
this case. English historians usually assume that
"Vikings" meant "men from the Vík" of Norway;
but the word does not seem to have been used in
this sense by saga-writers, who called the dwellers in
Vikin *Vikverskar* or *Vikverjar*, though in the mediæval
Icelandic Bishops' sagas *Suðvíkingr* means a man from
Súðavík, *Vestfolding* a man from Vestfold, and so on.
The word *víkingr* means in the Sagas any pirate, of
whatever nationality. For instances, the rather early
Kormáks-saga, relating adventures of a party of
Icelanders and a German, calls them all "vikings,"
and *Landnámabók* gives the name to any Scandinavian
sea-rovers. Nor does it mean "haunting the creeks
of England, the lochs of Scotland and the loughs of
Ireland;" for though it is true that there is no word
austr-víking (piracy in the east) parallel to *vestr-víking*
(piracy in the west), still Egil's saga (chap. 36) tells
how "they went in *víking* on the eastern way," to
Russia. The word *víking* (feminine) means the
life of a pirate, a free-booting voyage; "to go in

viking," is a common phrase and one used before the sagas were written down, for a Swedish runic stone records a man who " died on the west voyage in viking." The use of the word *viking* relates to occupation: the peaceful merchant, though he came from the same home and sailed into the same waters as the pirate, was not called a viking ; the distinction comes out in the description of one who was both by turns (*Egil's saga,* chap. 32) ; Björn was a great traveller, *var stundum i viking enn stundum i kaupferðum*—" he was sometimes in viking but sometimes on trading voyages." At first the name was honourable : " Naddodd was a great viking," says *Landnáma ;* but gradually as things became more settled it was possible for the pirate to be no hero ; " Thorbjörn bitra was a viking and a rascal," says *Landnáma* (ii. 32) of one who disgraced his calling by plundering the wrong people.   In the saga of Cormac the Skald the transition is apparent : the ancestors of the family were vikings of the good old sort in the ninth and early tenth centuries, but towards the close of the tenth century, when certain travellers on a trip from Trondhjem to Denmark were taken by " vikings," the word means simply pirates of no heroic sort.   *Rauðavíkingr,* a red pirate, is parallel to *rauða-rán,* red robbery ; and when the literature of the north began to be composed, and not only written down, by churchmen, to whom the deeds of their ancestors were as abhorrent as their heathenism, viking came to mean any robber ; until at last, in the story of David, the giant Goliath is called "this

cursed viking." But in the tenth century the common
noun had become already a proper name, as did
Dubhgall, Finngall, Lagman, Lochlann, and Sumarlidi ; there is a place in the south of Iceland called
Víkingslækr, Viking's brook, named in *Landnáma* ·
(v. 5, 6) in connexion with the settlement ; and later
the personal name of Viking is found on runic stones.
The inference is that the English word was adopted
quite early by the Scandinavians to denote the
honourable employment of the free buccaneer and
not as a geographical designation.

The employment was not without honour. To us,
looking back on the weary waste of life and the means
of life, estimating in imagination the wanton destruction of art and literature, the sufferings of innocent
people massacred or driven into slavery among heathens
and barbarians, or left to struggle and starve in the
ruins of their homes, it is easy to understand the bitterness with which the Viking attacks were regarded, and
the despair of the litany : " A furore Normannorum,
libera nos, Domine." But it is easy also to forget that
the bitterness was felt because the Vikings were heathen
and barbarians, a despised race, regarded in the ninth
century as, in the twelfth century, Saracens abroad and
Jews at home were regarded. When in Christian Ireland monks fought with monks, and kings made war
on priests and women, it was the normal course of
nature ; but that Gentiles should come in and poach
upon the preserves of royal sportsmen was the un-
bearable shame. In England for many a year stout
resistance was made ; the Vikings were often beaten,

and sometimes treated with greater cruelty than they intended to inflict.   There is no trace, in the earlier period, of needless cruelty on their part, except the fact, which seems needless to us but was by no means so in that age, of their making any such attacks at all. It was only later, by contact with the South, that they learnt to torture ; but we cannot say that they met easy deaths when they were captured (see for example page 68).[1] Nor was their life easy; hard fare, heavy labour at the oar, exposure in open boats to all the storms of the North, difficult navigation of unknown seas, comfortless and homeless wanderings in hostile lands,—the fate of a galley-slave in everything but freedom and the chances of glory and gold.

It was not a heroic life, as we count heroism to-day. The thirst for gold, torn from fine reliquaries and shrines and the jewelled covers of psalm-books, to be hammered into arm-rings or hoarded in holes, seems childish to a modern reader ; and the traffic in slaves, which formed the largest and most lucrative part of the Viking's booty, shocks our sentiments.   But in the ninth century the Viking could plead ample precedent ; he was only doing what the most civilised were doing ; his fault was that he did it rather more skilfully.   For indeed he was, in his time, the most capable of mankind ; not fully matured, but not without his own high civilisation, having more than the rudiments of domestic comforts and graces, more than

---

[1] Also see a paper by Mr. H. St. G. Gray, on "Danes' Skins on Church Doors" ; *Saga-book of the Viking Club*, V.

the elements of the finer arts and crafts, by which, if
by anything, a race is judged.   He was law-abiding,
beyond most; intelligent and ready to learn, so that the
story of captive Greece capturing her conquerors was
often repeated, when the sea-rover settled in Ireland,
or England, or France.   He was, in a word, the man
who deserved a hearing and who made himself heard.
And if he knew nothing as yet of the faith in which
Columba and Bede had so beautifully spent their
lives, he was, in higher moments, by no means a soul-
less savage.   In one of the Edda songs, *Hyndluljöd*,
there is a verse which we may fancy was sung to himself by many a young adventurer, as the boat tossed in
the breakers in sight of white cliffs and the unknown
fate in store :—

Victory He giveth, and wealth—at His will ;
Wisdom and words—they may win them who can :
As He gives the boat breeze so He gives the skald skill,
But to each giveth Odin the heart of a man.

Now it was some twenty years after the outbreak of
the Saxon war (p. 58) and seven years or more after the
attacks of "wicked men" on the Channel coasts, that
we have the first serious incident of the Viking Age,
the sack of Lindisfarne, in January, 793.   It was
heralded by storms, lightnings and "fiery dragons in
the air" (*i. e.* aurora borealis).   Symeon of Durham
pauses in his rapid *History of the Kings* to describe the
island with its curious sands and tides, and the noble
monastery once ruled by St. Cuthbert, and then paints
at length the landing of the Gentiles like wolves, slaying flocks and herds, priests and Levites, monks and

E

nuns: trampling the holy places, throwing down the altars, pillaging the treasuries. "Some of the monks they killed; a large number they carried away captive; the greater part they thrust out stripped and insulted; a few were drowned." The witness of the chroniclers is confirmed by a letter of Alcuin's of 794, showing that the news reached the Continent and created no little panic. But the extraordinary circumstance is that the landing was made on the 8th of January. It is true that the North Sea is sometimes sunny and calm in the depth of winter, but this had been a particularly stormy season. Later Vikings chose the summer for their excursions, and *sumarliði*, "summer-sailor," was synonymous with "pirate." Cattle and sheep, in that age, were slaughtered in autumn, and only a few stock beasts kept to be fed on hay through the winter; so that the flocks and herds on Lindisfarne (*jumenta, oves et boves*) could not have been more than sufficed for the *strandhögg*, the slaughter by the shore, for the feast which was the usual finish to a raid. The raiders had not come for cattle, but for gold and slaves; they knew where to get what they wanted—at a rich monastery on an island to which help from the surrounding country would be slow in coming; and they knew what to do with the slaves when they had captured them. We are told that Scandinavia was over-populated, and even if that was not the case, it was hardly necessary to import labour into Denmark, still less into Norway; a monk or a nun from England would be little use on a fell-side farm in Hardanger or Sogn. There must have been recognised markets in Flanders

and France for such commodities; later on, captives
were sold in Ireland or carried east to Esthonia and
Russia. But in January 793 a cargo of English monks
could not have been taken so far with profit, and
there is no hint here or elsewhere that the Vikings
took prisoners with the definite intention of holding
them to ransom, except in a much later period when
all the circumstances had changed, as in the sack of
Canterbury, 1012. They carried off their captives to
sell in some distant port; but where?

Everything seems to indicate that this attack came
from the south. We have hints of previous plundering on French and English coasts, and Roger de
Hoveden, a north-country writer, says that before the
attack on Lindisfarne there had been attempts on
the Northumbrian coast. The earlier Scandinavian
boat, long and shallow and with great, top-heavy sail
was not built for crossing the North Sea in winter.
Alcuin indeed wrote, "Nothing like their mode of
navigation has ever been heard of before," and the
adventure was in any case a remarkable achievement.
Still the coast route must have been the one followed
on this occasion; and the sudden, decisive attack
upon the weakest point, the rich, undefended island,
showed previous knowledge and a well-laid plan of
action. We cannot help feeling that the "wolves"
were led by a fox whose earth lay somewhere nearer
than Norway or even Denmark; and that as Christian
nations had set the example of raiding, so now a
"Christian" employer showed the way and profited
by the work—some one at least who lived in a country

nominally under the rule of the Christian emperor. The first viking raids were not a war of heathenism in revenge for the oppression of the Old Saxons; they were a new form of sport, at the back of which were "business interests;" and Danes, not Norse, were concerned.

Next year "the aforesaid Pagans" tried to repeat their success. They returned and ravaged Ecgfrid's port and the monastery at Done-mouth—Jarrow, where the little Don joins the Tyne. "But St. Cuthbert did not let them depart unpunished. Indeed their chief was slain by the English on the spot *with a cruel death*, and after a short space of time the violence of a tempest shook, ruined and brake to pieces their ships; and very many the sea overwhelmed. Some were cast ashore, and soon killed without pity. And this served them right for doing grave harm to those who had never done them harm" (Symeon).

Under 792 (correctly 794) the Ulster Annals note with evident exaggeration, "all the coast of Britain ravaged by the foreigners;" and, two years later, "the foreigners ravage Fortrenn (central Scotland) and distress the Picts." This may mean that, in spite of the reverse at Jarrow, the raids were pushed farther north, up the east coast of Britain. It is not proved that Vikings had reached the south-west of Scotland in 796.

The year 795, in which the Vikings did not venture back to the scene of the disaster of 794, was spent in an attempt in another direction. A party sailed round

the south coast and made a descent on Glamorganshire (*Gwentian Chronicle*), where the peninsula of
Gower was often afterwards the scene of their land-
ings, and then sailed across St. George's Channel to
the Irish coast, which they followed until they came
to another island monastery, Lambey, then known as
Rechru (genitive Rechrainn, the name used by Moore
in the hog-drowning story quoted p. 48). Here they
"burnt, spoiled and impoverished the shrines" of the
abbey founded by St. Columba. Some identify this
place with Rachaire or Rathlin island, co. Antrim.

A letter of Alcuin, written in 797, speaks of the
ravages as continuing; and in 798 a second invasion
of the Irish Sea was made. Following, no doubt, the
same route, they again made for a rich island monastery, the Celtic shrine of St. Dochonna on St. Patrick's
Island (Holm Peel), on the west coast of Man. Skye
is named as attacked about this time, but the small
Columban monastery in the south of that island is
hardly likely to have been attacked, either from the
north or the south, without any attempt being made
to gather in the riches of Iona—so near at hand and
so much more tempting. Skye and Iona must have
suffered about the same time, namely in 802.

Meanwhile, in 799 and 800, France and Frisia had
occupied the attention of the pirates. If at first, as
we suspect, the Vikings had received help and en-
couragement from France or Frisia, it did not prevent
their turning to those districts in the years when they
left Ireland and England to lie fallow. The sequence
of their descents proves that all these attacks came

from the same quarter:—793, Lindisfarne ; 794,
Jarrow ; 795, Rechru ; 796, East-coast of Scotland ;
797, Alcuin's notice of continued ravages ; 798, Peel,
Isle of Man ; 799, France ; 800, Frisia ; 802, Iona.
These were no chance landfalls of semi-savage rovers,
but a definite scheme to exploit the most available
material.   Where good resistance was offered, no
further attempts were made : after the disaster at
Jarrow there is no record of a descent on English
ground for nearly 40 years ; it was not worth while.
The finding of English coins of the early " eight-
twenties " in county Wicklow has been thought to
indicate that in those years Vikings from Ireland made
unrecorded raids on south-eastern England : but it is
possible that these English coins were brought to
Ireland by way of trade, for at the time there was no
Irish coinage, whereas trade always went on.   And in
spite of Viking attacks life went on ; the burnt thatch
was renewed, the desecrated altar reconsecrated, and
in the case of so famous a centre as Iona the offerings
of the faithful soon replaced the loss.   How well this
was known to the managers of the Viking enterprise
we can see from the fact that in four years the abbey
was worth robbing again, and in 806 a second attack
was made.   This time the monks tried to defend
their treasures, and sixty-eight were slain in the
fight.

Next year the pirates, doubtless the same party
and under the same auspices, sailed round the north
coast of Ireland into Donegal Bay, and plundered
Inishmurry, yet another rich island monastery, whose

curious remains of early architecture are still to be seen (*Scotland in Early Christian Times*, i. p. 87). After that, for several years there is a cessation of raids; Godfred, king of Denmark, was employing all hands in war with the Slavs, with Frisia and with Charlemagne. But after his death we find that the Vikings at once returned to Ireland. In 811–813 they began a new phase of their operations, as though the experience of the late war had taught them—the most teachable of people—how to do more than fall upon a defenceless island and fly with the plunder. They now landed and went up the country, in Ulster, in Connemara, and to the lakes of Killarney. They were not always successful, for both the Irish annals and Eginhard tell us that they were beaten off with great loss, more than once. These disasters appear to have disheartened them; for seven years there are no more invasions.

At last we have come to the period when we begin to hear of Norwegians in North British seas. That they had some knowledge of the route, and perhaps occasionally used it in fishing or trading voyages, is very likely; indeed it would be inconceivable that this piece of water between Shetland and Norway was untraversed when the route to the Færoes and Iceland was well known to the Irish. It seems reasonable to suppose that the example of the Danish enterprises was talked about, and soon followed, by the men of Hordaland; the contagion of enterprise, so to speak, spread northward. But there was a difference from the beginning between the Danish and the Norwegian incursions. The Danes came chiefly for plunder, and returned to their own sunny and fertile country to enjoy the fruits of their industry; while the Norse, living in a ruder climate, more straitened for the means of life in their narrow fields along the fjord-sides, and less spoiled by commerce with the rich south, came to find new homes in milder and more spacious regions. To them the North of Britain, and still more the coasts of the Irish Sea, were southern lands : they could never have found in the bee-hive huts and rude oratories of the Orkneys and the northern Hebrides that wealth of plunder which attracted the first Vikings to Lindisfarne and Iona; but they found ready-made houses and cultivated fields, or the space they needed for expansion. Even the Færoes were colonised by the Norse fifty years before any settlement was effected by the Danes in England ; and if the methods of the two classes of Vikings were hardly distinguishable by the natives who resented their presence, their aims were not the same. It might be said, as a rough summing-up of the earlier Viking period, that the Danes showed the way westward to the Norse, but the Norse set the example of conquest and colonisation to the Danes. We shall see (p. 182 onward) that the most permanent foreign settlements on British soil were chiefly Norse in origin and character.

It was perhaps owing to the rivalry created by the earlier Norse invasions that the Danish attacks began again in 820 or 822. They had the same object, gold and slaves. From Edar, which they called *Höf ð i*, Howth, they carried off "a great prey of women," and in 823 plundered Inis-dowill (Inch, co. Wexford) and Cork; then, sailing along the coast, climbed the almost inaccessible crags of Skellig Mhichel on the Kerry coast (where wonderful structures of this period still remain in the island cashel and beehive cells), and kidnapped the hermit Eitgall, " et cito mortuus est fame et siti,"—perhaps set ashore as a useless captive, for on board the ships he need not have starved to death. Next year the famous monastery of Bangor (co. Down) was sacked; "the oratory was broken, and the relics of Comhgall were shaken from the shrine, as Comhgall himself had foretold."

A year later they made the third attack on Iona, where the monastery, which in 818 had been rebuilt in stone on a new site, was once more plundered. The occasion is marked by the death of Blathmac mac Flainn, and by the account of it written by Walafrid Strabo, abbot of Augiadives (Reichenau on the Lake of Constance), who himself died only twenty-one years afterwards. Blathmac seems to have expected the chance of his death sooner or later at the hands of Vikings; though the rebuilding of the monastery suggests that the Columban brotherhood thought the storm was over, after five years had passed without sign of piracy from the south, and obviously without sign of Norse attacks from the north. When at last the sails of the approaching fleet were seen from the look-out on Dunii, the jewelled golden shrine that held the sacred relics of Columba was hastily buried, and most of the monks fled to hiding-places on the moors of the island. Some few remained to resist, and were slain. Blathmac stood to his post at the altar, saying mass, until he was seized and required to give up the treasure—for the Vikings were well aware of its existence; they had not come without information. He on his part knew enough about the strangers to reply in their language. This may mean that he had studied Danish, or that a few words of English sufficed; for no doubt Blathmac spoke English as many an educated Irishman must have spoken it, and as, *vice versa*, Englishmen like Kings Oswiu and Aldfrith spoke Gaelic. He protested that he did not know where the treasure was hidden, but added that, if he did, he would not tell; whereupon they cut him down, and he attained his desire of martyrdom.

In the little building called St. Columba's tomb, close to the west end of the cathedral of Iona, there are two stone cists, which Skene thought, on the analogy of a similar oratory at Temple Molaga in Ireland, must have been made to contain the most valued of the relics. If so, that on the south must have held the bones of St. Columba, and as Walafrid especially mentions a miracle-working shrine of St. Blathmac, the cist on the north side of the cell may have been made as the coffin of the martyr.

With 825, the year of Grím Kamban in the Færoes, while Dicuil was finishing his book in France, began the serious and strenuous attempt on the inland shrines of Ireland. Downpatrick, Moville, Inisdowill, and Lusk suffered first (825–826), and then we find Vikings fighting the tribal chiefs up-country, sometimes defeated with slaughter, and yet persistent, until, in 832, Armagh was thrice plundered in one month, with many other churches, and the shrine of St. Adamnan was carried off from Donaghmoyne (co. Monaghan). Next year Niall, the new-made overking of Ireland, beat the Vikings at Derry, but they sacked Clondalkin. And all the while Irish kinglets and chiefs amused themselves at the old royal sport of ravage and massacre; so that the assaults of the Gaill are mere incidents, a small percentage in the catalogue of troubles. Even church-burning and monk-slaying were not unknown among the Irish; in this very year (833) the king of Cashel slaughtered the monks of Clonmacnois and Durrow; another chief had massacred the clergy of Kildare in the year before. Ireland was ripe for conquest, but since the beginning of their raids the Vikings had sailed past the coasts of England, year after year, and never made a landing serious enough for the chronicles to record.

Now, emboldened by success and experience, they extended the sphere of their adventures. The first great expedition against Flanders was made in 834, and then for three years they were plundering that coast and the coast of France to the mouth of the Loire. A few slight attacks were made upon England; a descent on Sheppey and a landing at Charmouth in Dorset, where they defeated the local forces, were episodes in the plundering on the other side of the

Channel. The case is different with the invasion of Cornwall in 838.

Ecgberht had conquered the West Welsh in 823, but they chafed under the yoke. Possibly by their invitation, or possibly as the first instance of a policy which was repeated a few years later in Brittany and in Ireland, the Vikings joined them. A great fleet came to Cornwall, and the army together with the Cornishmen marched eastward against Wessex. Ecgberht crossed the Tamar to meet them, and on Hengestesdune (perhaps Hengston Down, between Plymouth and Launceston) won a decisive victory.

The first plainly recorded name of a Viking chief is that of Saxulf, who is noticed in the Irish Annals as slain about 836. The next and greatest of this epoch is Turgesius, or Turgeis, formerly identified with the Thorgils, son of Harald Fairhair, mentioned by Snorri Sturluson, in spite of the hopeless anachronism. The name would stand for Thorgest, as Dr. Whitley Stokes suggested ; and Snorri's tale is no doubt a legend of his life, confused and misdated. The date of his arrival and the place of his origin are uncertain, but he seems to have been the first of the "foreigners" in Ireland who showed an intention to conquer the land and settle in it, perhaps somewhat earlier than 839, the date given for the advent of his "great royal fleet" in the *Wars of the Gaedhil with the Gaill*. He built a fort on Lough Ree, took Armagh, the chief centre of religion in the north of Ireland, and, according to the legend, made himself "abbot" of the monastery ; at the same time placing in Clonmacnois, the chief abbey of central Ireland, his wife Otta, where she sat on the altar of the church and "gave answers" in the character of a priestess or prophetess. At last he was captured by King Maelseachlann, and drowned in Lough Owel (co. Westmeath), in or about 843. A variant of the tale is given by Giraldus, and may perhaps have been known to Snorri, to the effect that he fell in love with a daughter of King Maelseachlann, and that she was sent to him with a company of fifteen young men dressed as girls, who stabbed him and his chiefs to death.

Thorgest may have been a Norwegian, for we get definite notice in the Irish Annals of the difference between Norse and Danes at the period of his arrival (see pp. 59, 60). But by the time of Thorgest's death Limerick had been founded as a Viking settlement, and Dublin (840) on a site captured in 836; while the colony in Wicklow (Wiking-law) was established at least as early as 835. About this time we have the first distinct notices of attempts to occupy southern and central Scotland, the hold of the Northmen on the Orkneys and Shetland being already secured. When Æthelwulf, the son of Ecgberht, came to the throne of Wessex, the aspect of affairs had altered from occasional predatory raids to determined invasion.

About 840 these new invasions began on the south coast of England; the first, repulsed from Southampton; the next at Portland, in which the Danes beat the Saxons by means of their trick of the feigned flight; the third, a successful raid upon Lindsey, East Anglia

and Kent; and the fourth, an attack on London and
Rochester, after which the Danes drew off to Cwenta-
wic (Étaples), and soon after sacked Rouen and
Nantes, in 845 besieging Paris. They returned to the
attack on England at Charmouth (Dorset) where
Æthelwulf himself, engaging the crews of thirty-five
Danish ships, was beaten. But the Danes then did
not follow up their success. At the mouth of the
Parret they were repulsed by the levies of Somerset
and Dorset, and again at " Wicganbeorh " in Dorset
in 851.

But by this time more serious efforts at conquest
were in preparation. In 850 a party landed on Thanet
(or on Sheppey) and wintered there, the first wintering
on English ground, and early next year a great fleet
of 350 ships sailed into the Thames; Canterbury and
London were sacked; Beorhtwulf of Mercia was put
to flight and died, perhaps of his wounds. Mr. Keary
(*The Vikings in Western Christendom*, p. 273) thinks
that this fleet was commanded by Rorik, one of the
family then ruling in Denmark. Rorik, if he was the
leader, hoped to found a kingdom of his own as other
leaders had done in Ireland : but there was more
resistance to be met with in the Saxons than in the
Celts. King Æthelwulf of Wessex fought the invaders
at Ockley in Surrey, and defeated them with great loss,
while his son Æthelstan, king of Kent, put out to
sea—the first indication of naval efforts on the part of
the Saxons—and won a battle off Sandwich, taking
nine ships and putting the rest to flight.

For a time the Danes fell back on the easier conquest of France, or tried England, as it were, by the back-door. They had formerly struck at Wessex through Cornwall; now they attempted the route through North Wales, perhaps trying to get the Welsh to co-operate as before. Æthelwulf gave his daughter in marriage to Burhred, the new king of Mercia, and joined him, at his request in 853, in an expedition against the Welsh, whom he reduced to subjection. That is to say, King Roderick ap Merfyn, between two fires, must have promised to expel the Vikings; and we find in the Ulster Annals, in 855, "Horm, chief of Black Gentiles, killed by Ruadhri mac Murminn, king of Wales"—the Orm who possibly gave their name to the Ormes Heads at Llandudno. The extent to which Orm's incursion had succeeded may be gathered from a Mercian charter of the same year, which mentions the fact that pagans had reached the district of the Wrekin (Birch, 487; Kemble, 277).

But while Æthelwulf was engaged in the west, the persistent Danes entered Thanet, and fought a battle with the men of Kent and Surrey, in which ealdorman Ealhere of Kent, who had won the sea-fight alongside of King Æthelstan at Sandwich, was slain. Two years later, Æthelwulf was again absent, trusting that all was quiet; but the Danes promptly came to winter in Sheppey.

He had gone on pilgrimage to Rome. On the way back he stayed three months with Charles the Bald. His first wife, the mother of Ælfred, appears to have died, and before leaving France he married Judith, daughter of Charles, a child of twelve. It can only

have been a nominal marriage of policy, for as he had
given his daughter to the Mercian king in order to
strengthen Wessex on the north against the Vikings, so
now he made an alliance with the Franks to secure as
far as possible the co-operation of the great southern
power in the same cause.   On his arrival home he
found his son Æthelbald in possession of the throne,
and thenceforward contented himself with the eastern
half of his old kingdom.   During his lifetime we hear of
no more Viking attacks ; his policy was successful, not
only for himself, but for Æthelbald, who succeeded
him, and the peace lasted into the days of Æthelberht,
the brother who followed.   So secure did the West-
Saxons feel, that when at last a body of Vikings, perhaps under Völund who was adventuring at this time
in France, suddenly landed and made a dash upon
Winchester, the capital city of the realm, it was only
after the storm and sack of the town that the local
fyrd was got together.   Then the Hampshire and
Berkshire men intercepted the raiders, and put them
to flight with great slaughter.   But the tide was
beginning to turn.

In 865 " the heathen army sat down in Thanet, and
made peace with the men of Kent, and the men of
Kent promised them money for the peace ; and during the peace and the promise of money, the army
stole away by night and ravaged all Kent to the eastward."   This is a noteworthy entry, for it marks the
first payment of the Danegeld which afterwards became such a burden to England ; and it is the first
example of the " Danish breach of faith " of which

so much is heard in later years—the usual cry of
those who are worsted in a sharp bargain. We
have no account of the Danish side of the story;
but now the conquest of the Danelaw had begun in
earnest.

F

II. THE DANELAW

THAT part of Britain which the Danes conquered in the days of King Ælfred was called in Anglo-Saxon *Denalagu*, the district in which the Danes' law prevailed. The word *lagu* in the sense of "laws" comes from the Scandinavian *lög*, which in its secondary use meant not only "laws," but the group of people who were ruled by a given code. *Gulathings lög*, or *Thrænda lög*, came to be almost geographical expressions for the country which owned the rulings of the Gulathing, or the neighbourhood of Trondhjem. Hence the form "Danelaw," used by recent historians as a convenient rendering of *Denalagu*, is not misleading, beside being more readable than the hybrid "Danelagh."

King Ælfred's life covers the period of this conquest, the second half of the ninth century. After the tentative attacks of the first sixteen years, came the invasion of the Great Army, which created the Danelaw, followed by the futile attempt of Hástein (Hasting) to settle in Ælfred's realm. By the year 900 the ethnological map of England had been drawn on lines which last, with alterations in details only, to this day. The story is one of stirring deeds on both sides.

If we admire the heroic defence of the Saxon king, we cannot forget that most of us who form the English nation have in our veins more than a little of the Viking blood. We owe our existence as much to one side as to the other, and it is a false patriotism and a mistaken view of history which asks us to give our sympathies exclusively to either party in this struggle of a thousand years ago. To tell the story fully in the limits of this work is impossible; we must, however, sketch the course of events in order to make the results intelligible.

When Æthelred, the fourth son of Ecgberht, succeeded to the throne, his accession was the signal for the beginning of troubles to which all previous incursions had been literally like ships that pass in the night. In that year 866, says Æthelwerd, "the fleets of the tyrant Hingwar arrived in England from the north,"—*de Danubio*, says Asser; *de Danubia*, Symeon copies him : from Denmark, of course— "and wintered among the East Angles; and having established their arms there, they got them horses, and made peace with all the inhabitants of their own neighbourhood." In other words, they became a force of wonderfully active and mobile mounted infantry, like the hobelars of the thirteenth century or the Boers of recent times; and their new policy was to conciliate the immediate neighbourhood in which they settled, in order to form a base of operations. This was a repetition of the policy already seen in Cornwall, Brittany and Wales; and now it seems to have been applied to East Anglia, where the natives—still

forming a separate kingdom, but a dependency—might
be stirred up to take part in attacks on the power which
had robbed them of the supremacy they boasted in the
days of Redwald. Their king, afterwards known as
St. Eadmund the Martyr, is not mentioned in these
transactions ; when his turn came he fought his fight
and suffered his fate with a courage no less than that
of the greatest hero of the Sagas. There was no lack
of courage in England, but there was one thing need-
ful—the master-mind, which had not yet shown itself
here. We cannot but suspect, however, that on the
side of the Vikings there was one who, if we knew more
about him, would deserve mention with the Hannibals
and Napoleons of history.

When we consider the strategy of these invaders,
the great war-game which was going on ; how fleet
after fleet sought the weakest points ; how, on the
failure of frontal attack, new attacks were made in
flank ; how the diplomacy of alliance with discontented
dependencies was followed ; how the maxim of " divide
and conquer " was understood ; how the net was drawn
around England from point to point on either hand,
until the time came for the final effort that should
strangle the power of Wessex and make the British
Islands wholly Scandinavian :—when we consider this,
it is impossible to escape the idea that some great
plan was in operation, some strong mind directing a
warfare which, however originated, had become no
casual scramble of independent adventurers, nor even
an organisation merely to exploit their sporting in-
stincts, but a resolute scheme of conquest played with

the skill of a chess-player on the field of empire. It
was not for nothing that the Vikings on board their
ships played draught-games ; one finds their travelling
chessboards and tenoned pieces, showing how they
beguiled the time in rough weather with something
more intellectual than drinking and horseplay. The
same tendency marks their art and literature. Anglo-
Saxon poetry has imagination ; the verse of the
Northmen, in its intricate metres and rhymes, its
elaboration of synonyms and "kennings," has in
genuity to equal any art of the kind before or since.
Anglo-Saxon sculpture has grace and charm learnt
from abroad, but soon degenerating ; while Scandinavian ornament develops from simple models into
labyrinths of intricacy compared with which even the
cobweb lace of Celtic design, being regular and needing
more patience than thought, is easy to follow. The
success of the Vikings was by no means a success of
rude and savage force ; it was a triumph of mental
power as well as of moral endurance and physical
bravery.

Their armour and weapons are noted in *The Wars
of the Gaedhil and the Gaill* as superior to those of
the Irish, who were no mean craftsmen. At the siege
of Paris they seem to have used machines and methods
of assault as good as those employed for several centuries to follow ; and in the campaign of Ivar they
fortified themselves in earthworks—not mere boundary
dykes like the Danework—the use of which was
unusual in Scandinavia until the burg of the Jómsvi-
kings gave an example of the skill they learnt in their

southern campaigns. The adoption of the mounted
infantry system, afterwards copied by the English, put
them at once into a position of great tactical advantage ; just as their well-known but most difficult trick
of the feigned flight enabled them to break the line of
the bravest Saxon fyrd, fighting on the old hand-to-
hand principles. Odin, in far antiquity, as their
stories told, taught his children the " swine-fylking,"
—the charge in wedge-formation, such as the High-
landers used at Prestonpans ; but who was the new
culture-hero who made use of many experiences
gathered from the South, and sent out the Vikings
of the ninth century to be the most efficient soldiery
of their age ? Who planned the great campaign by
which East Anglia, Deira and Mercia, were success-
ively annexed ? and why did he fail to annex the
kingdom of Ælfred ?

The genius of Viking conquest, according to Prof. A.
Bugge (*Vikingerne*, i. p. 139) was Thorgest, who fell in
Ireland in 843 after extending his empire over half the
country. But a greater man may be suspected in the
half-mythical Ivar " the Boneless," who in 857 to 862
had been fighting in Ireland, and now led the great
host through all its wonderful successes, only to disappear from the scene at the moment before the tide
turned, and the good fortune of the Saxons prevailed.
It was he whom the Irish Annals called " chief king
of all Northmen in Britain and Ireland," and the
English chroniclers name with deepest hate, the
tribute of the conquered. In the Sagas he is the
wily one, " who had no bones in his body, but was

very wise ;" who succeeded in each enterprise by craft,
when the courage of his brothers had failed. Eldest
of the sons of Ragnar Lodbrok by the daughter of
Sigurd the dragon-slayer, he is the one constant
factor in the varying groups of conquerors, as given
by different sources. His brothers in Ragnar's Saga
are Sigurd Snake-eye, Hvítserk and Björn Ironside ;
in the English chroniclers, Halfdan and Hubba (Ubbi),
though Symeon distinguishes the last as Dux Frisi-
orum ; in the Annals of Roskilde, Ubi, Björn and
Ulph ; and in the Irish *Three Fragments*, Olaf the
White and Oisla (Háisl). He appears 866–870 as
directing operations in England, Scotland and Ireland,
always with success ; and though the saga-leaves him
childless, he must be the father of the great line of
Dublin kings, and the "Old Ivar of the Judgments"
who appears at the head of Hebridean clan-pedigrees.

The rapidity of the conquest, when Ivar took it in
hand, is remarkable. So far, the Vikings had made
no headway ; now, five years sufficed for the complete
and permanent subjugation of East Anglia, Deira
and northern Mercia : and this was not because
no resistance, or a poor resistance, was offered. It
is true that Northumbria was disturbed by faction ;
king Osberht had been dethroned by a usurper Ælla,
and this was Ivar's opportunity ; but, unlike the Irish,
the Anglian factions sunk their differences and united
in fierce opposition to the common enemy. Mercia
was a strong power, and had support from Wessex,
but nothing stood against Ivar. Wessex was saved by
Ælfred, but only after Ivar was gone.

In the spring of 867 the Great Army rode across the Humber, and on November 1 had taken York. On March 21, 868, all Northumbria joined in an attack on their position, and utterly failed. If it had been Ivar's object to ravage, he would have overrun Bernicia; if he had wished to destroy, he would not have left the great churches at York and Ripon standing. Shrines were plundered, but the land was left under a native king, one Ecgberht, who—either as a downright renegade or in the hope of restoring some order from the wreck—consented to hold it as the Danes' tributary. Thus he founded a lasting dynasty.

Ivar's plan was to clear the board of Mercia, and to put Wessex in check. He seized Nottingham : Burhred slowly called out his forces, and called in help from Æthelred and Ælfred; but the only result was a treaty under which Ivar returned leisurely to York, and fortified the city anew in the winter of 869, 870. Their almost Roman habit of entrenching a position was a fresh feature in English warfare, learnt perhaps from the Carlovingian empire, and imitated by Ælfred; for, as Asser says, the old walls of York were poor defences.

In 870 Ivar's army, avoiding central Mercia, and so far respecting the treaty of Nottingham, marched through Lincolnshire to intrench itself at Thetford. King Eadmund of East Anglia attacked it in vain, and fell; some accounts tell us that he was slain in battle; the later legend of his martyrdom is well known. But if the tale of cruelty is true, the only explanation, at this period, would be that he was regarded by Ivar as a traitor to the charge which, like Ecgberht in Northumbria, he may have undertaken under the Danes. We have no mention of his father, or pedigree connecting him with native kings. But at least he fell in defence of his country and faith, and earned the crown of martyrdom. His feast day fixes the date as November 20, 870.

From that moment forth, Ivar too disappears from England. He is usually represented as the chief actor in the death of St. Eadmund, but in all subsequent operations he is not named. The Annals of Ulster, which often antedate by a year, mention under 869 "The siege of Alclyde (Dumbarton) by the Northmen: Olaf and Ivar, two kings of the Northmen, besieged that stronghold, and at the end of four months they stormed and sacked it;" and then, next year, that Olaf (the White) and Ivar came again to Dublin from Scotland "and a very great spoil of captives, *English*, British and Pictish, was carried away to Ireland;" and finally, under 872, "Ivar, King of the Northmen of all Ireland and Britain, ended his life." There can be no doubt that this Ivar is the man who led the army in England: he would not otherwise have been described as king of the Northmen of all Ireland and Britain; nor would he have been able to carry to Dublin "a very great spoil of *English* captives" as well as of British (or Strathclyde Welsh) who were taken at the sack of Dumbarton, the chief stronghold of Strathclyde. It is curious to find him acting with Olaf the White, a Norseman; but he had been with him before in 858 and 862, and

then disappeared from Irish annals until now. Ivar
the Crafty probably made light of the differences
between Black and White Gaill, when the chance
offered for pushing his fortunes ; and now, seeing the
conquest of England going forward, and affairs of his
cause in the North hanging in the balance by the
long siege of the Strathclyde capital, hastened to lend
his aid, bringing his army and English spoil.

The siege over, and after the winter on the Clyde,
he sailed for Dublin, and died there in peace two years
later.   One MS. of the Annals makes the startling
statement " he slept in Christ."   Is it possible, one
is tempted to ask, that the clearest-headed and the
thoughtfullest of all the Viking leaders found, before
his death, something unperceived before in the religion
he had persecuted ? It is not so entirely inconceivable,
for in Dublin the old king must have seen much of
Queen Aud, the wife of Olaf the White ; she was then
a woman of early middle age, for she died in 900,
advanced in years ; and she was known as one of the
Christian settlers in Iceland, and as one of the most
forceful characters in Old Northern history.   But we
must not build on a word which, after all, may be a
clerical error.

When Ivar left the army in England it had all
the old enterprise and fire ; the scheme of conquest
was pursued, but no further decisive and permanent
successes were gained.   What was afterwards the
Danelaw was now occupied ; nothing more was added
n spite of the strenuous warfare of the next seven
years : the master-mind was gone.

Halfdan, said to be Ivar's brother, after the winter
was out, prepared to finish the work by invading
Wessex. With him was King Bagsecg or Bægsceg,
Sigtrygg the Old and Sigtrygg the Young, Osbjörn,
Fræna, and Harald, all named as jarls who fell in this
campaign. They set out about Christmas-tide, 870.
At this period the Chronicles begin the year with
Christmas, and the dates of their earlier movements
are precise enough to give the days on which the
actions were fought (see the Rev. C. Plummer's *Life
and Times of Alfred the Great*, p. 93). As they came
from Thetford after many months of land operations,
it is not likely that they took boats up the Thames :
probably they rode along the Icknield way, making
for Winchester. Near the Thames they must have
been aware of the Wessex army on the watch, for the
rapidity with which they were attacked shows that
they were not unexpected.

At Reading there was a royal vill and a little
monastery to plunder. There was also a fine site
for a fortress, in the tongue of land between Thames
and Kennet ; for at that time the land now covered
by the railway-stations was marsh, and the tip of
the tongue, now occupied by Huntley & Palmer's
biscuit factory, was close to navigable water from
which boats could go down the river and out to sea.
Asser has puzzled historians by saying that the town
was south of the Thames, but that the Danes made a
dyke between the two rivers to the right (south) of
the town (or vill). Now the Saxon monastery seems
to have been where St. Mary's stands, and no dyke

from Thames to Kennet could be south of the town, unless the town were on the Forbury (perhaps *Forn-borg*, "ancient fort"). The Danes' dyke is probably the Vastern dyke of old maps, running round the Abbey precincts and northward to the Vastern, which may have been a *vatz-tjörn*, "water-tarn"); while the Clappers (*klappir*, " stepping stones ") was the ford of the Thames at Caversham Lock. It would be curious if the short occupation fixed Norse names to this Wessex site, but there was a Danish occupation of the Thames Valley in the eleventh century also.

From December 28, 870, the Danes made Reading their headquarters for about twelve months. On Dec. 31, the Berkshire men cut up a party of foragers at Englefield ; on Jan. 4, 871, Æthelred and Ælfred attacked the camp and fought a battle—probably on the spot where the Reading market-place now stands—but were driven off with loss ; on Jan. 8, they intercepted a strong force of Danes out for reconnaissance along the Ridgeway, and won the victory of Ashdown. At Basing, Jan. 22, the Vikings beat them, and again on March 22, at Meretune (site disputed). Æthelred was perhaps wounded in this battle ; he died April 24, leaving the kingdom to his young brother Ælfred.

Halfdan, however, contented himself with foraging, while he waited for reinforcements. He fought many minor battles ; Æthelwerd the chronicler reckons three fights during the summer of 871, in which eleven more jarls of the Danes were slain ; Asser counts eight battles in the whole campaign, with the loss of one king and nine jarls. But at last Halfdan abandoned the struggle, and retired to London. As the Vikings in 879 had a camp at Fulham, perhaps the earthworks which enclose the Bishop's palace and the mound within the ramparts (described by Mr. G. M. Atkinson in a paper read to the Viking Club, 1907) may have been Halfdan's camp. Ælfred kept his men in the field, but Burhred paid an enormous Danegeld and induced the Vikings to spare London. They marched to Torksey on the Trent, and then wintered at Repton. Burhred left his kingdom in despair, and died at Rome. In his place the Danes set up Ceolwulf, an Englishman, another instance of their not unenlightened policy. One would expect that there were many adventurers who would have been pleased to sit on the throne of Mercia, but in that case an army of occupation would have been needed, and the forces at Halfdan's disposal would have been weakened. As it was, the Danes had now to occupy East Anglia and Deira with numbers diminished by a long and unsuccessful campaign. Early in 875 the army divided. One part under Halfdan took up winter quarters on the Tyne, and raided the shrines of Bernicia, marched through Cumberland, and attacked the Picts (of Galloway); under that date the Ulster Annals also mention "a great slaughter of Picts by Dubhgalls." It is assumed by J. R. Green (*Conquest of England*, p. 107) that Halfdan went further north, to attack King Constantine, who, according to a chronology which is hardly tenable (see pp. 225, 248), is represented as fighting

Thorstein, son of Olaf the White, and Jarl Sigurd of Orkney; but the former kingdom of Northumberland had included Galloway, and it is likely that Halfdan's object was to extend his power to the ancient borders of his realm. Next year he "dealt out the lands of Northumbria, and they thenceforth continued ploughing and tilling them."

The other part of the great army under Guthorm, Asketil and Hámund, went in 875 to winter at Cambridge. So far, they might be supposed to have burnt their ships, for all three campaigns had been on land, but their ships were soon called into action. Ælfred in person fought a naval battle off the south coast, and won it; but in 876 Guthorm sailed round to Poole harbour to join the army of Ubbi from Wales. Asser tells how he seized "the castellum," ancient square earthworks, "called Wareham, where there is a convent of nuns, between the two rivers Frome and Trent." Ælfred bought peace, and the Danes swore on the Holy Ring that they would depart; but early in 877 they sallied out by night and rode to Exeter. Ælfred could only blockade them, and set his ships to watch the mouth of the Exe. An interpolator of Asser (c. 50; ed. Stevenson, p. 39) says that he had ships built in all parts of his kingdom, and placed "pirates" on board to fight the Danes: but the phrase is so vague and rhetorical that we must not assume that these man-of-war's men were Norse, brought in to fight their rivals.

The Danish fleet of 120 sail coming from Wareham to force the blockade was wrecked off Swanage, and the Saxons massacred the survivors. Offers of peace were renewed, and the army withdrew to Gloucester, and then to Chippenham, where they spent the early months of 878. The inhabitants of the district who could do so fled into Wales, and the west country was entirely in the hands of the Vikings.

This is the time when Ælfred is said to have burnt the cakes. As a matter of fact he was reduced to taking refuge among the fens of Athelney; not that he was wholly inactive, but he had with him only his personal retinue and the Somerset fyrd under ealdorman Æthelnoth. It is extraordinary to us to think of the other shires of Wessex sitting at home and taking no steps for the rescue of those whom we should now consider their fellow-country-men; but there was no united "England" in those days, when each district had until recently been independent, and still retained its local jealousies. It is the great praise of Ælfred that he overcame this feeling among the various groups of the people he ruled, and created the possibility of efficient fighting power in a country which, for all its civilisation and Christianity, was behind the pagans in political and military organisation.

At the junction of the Tone and the Parret the triple-ramparted mound called Borough Mump may be the fort in Athelney built by King Ælfred; the *Arx Cynuit*, held by the men of Devon against Ubbi and the Danes is a site about which there has been much dispute. Here a signal victory was won over the Vikings, and their Raven standard was captured.

In May 878 Ælfred sent word to the men of Somerset,
Wilts, and Hampshire, met them on the east of
Selwood forest, and, after a day's march, fell suddenly
on the Vikings at Ethandune.[1] His victory ended
the campaign ; Guthorm was baptised, taking the
name of Æthelstan, and removed the army to East
Anglia, 879.

In 884 a Danish host, which had left Fulham in
879 for the Continent, returned, and besieged Rochester, but were driven off. There seems to have been
help given them by the Danes in East Anglia, and
after some sea-fighting a treaty was made, commonly
but inaccurately cited as the Frith of Wedmore, fixing
the boundary. It was to run up the Thames and the
sea to a point near Hertford, thence to Bedford, and
up the Ouse to Watling Street, near Stony Stratford.
This gave London to Wessex, perhaps as a compen-
sation for the breach of the previous treaty.

Ælfred had learnt in his struggle with Guthorm
the impossibility of meeting sudden invasion with
slowly gathered and temporary local levies, and he
arranged for relays of militia, "so that one-half was
constantly at home, and the other in the field, beside
those whose duty it was to defend the burgs." He
had observed the mobility of the Danes, and we find

[1] The circumstances of this campaign and the identification
of the sites present questions which cannot be dealt with here.
Valuable contributions to the subject are given in Mr. W. H.
Stevenson's notes to Asser's *Life of Ælfred*, pp. 262–278 :
another line is taken by the Rev. C. W. Whistler in the *Saga-book
of the Viking Club*, ii., pp. 153–197, and the controversy is
hardly at an end as yet.

him putting his men on horseback; he began to fortify
and garrison important points, and he continued im-
proving his fleet.   Consequently, when Hástein came,
circumstances were far less favourable to his enterprise
than they would have been twenty years earlier; and
not even his army of veterans, highly organised, well
equipped, and thoroughly trained as they were, could
succeed where Halfdan and Guthorm had failed.   He
was a daring adventurer; his exploits in Spain and
the Mediterranean read like a romance (see C. F.
Keary, *The Vikings in Western Christendom*, pp. 320–
326), and in France he had been the terror of the
Loire for twenty years.   Of late he had moved to
Flanders, with his head-quarters at Louvain.   He
came to England, not with the great designs of Ivar,
but rather through necessity; being beaten with a
signal defeat on the Dyle (Sept. 1, 891), and starved
out by the famine of 892, he was forced to seek a new
home.

In the autumn of 892 a fleet of 250 ships came over
from Boulogne to the Roman Portus Lemanis and up
the river Limen (then in existence) to Appledore, in
Kent.   There the Vikings found a fort in process of
building, which they seized and completed.   Soon
afterwards Hástein himself with 80 ships entered the
Thames, and fortified a position at Milton, near
Sittingbourne.   Ælfred tried to forestall interfer-
ence by exacting pledges—which proved in vain—
that East Anglia and Northumbria would not help
the invaders.   He negotiated with Hástein, who
allowed his sons to be baptised, but refused—or was

G

unable—to leave the country. Early in April the
Danes at Appledore tried to reach their friends in
East Anglia by a route west of the Weald, but the
Saxons continuing to regard them as enemies, pursued and drove them to take refuge in the island of
Thorney, near West Drayton. Guthorm sent a fleet
to attack Exeter ; and, from some port in Lancashire
or Cumberland held by the Northumbrian Danes,
another fleet came to the North Devon coast. Both
invasions were repulsed, and the Danes in Thorney
succeeded in joining their friends in East Anglia,
whither Hástein followed them. He built the burg at
Benfleet, called by Æthelwerd Danasuda (*Dana-suð*,
the "Danes' clinch": *suð* being the clinched outer
boarding of a house or planking of a ship). When
this was stormed in his absence, he built a new burg
at Shoebury, and then marched up the Thames and
across country, in the hope of finding in Wales the
home denied in England. At Buttingdune (Butting-
ton, near Welshpool; see a paper by Mr. C. W.
Dymond, Powysland Club, 1900) he was besieged and
defeated. The survivors rode back to Essex, but
before long their pressing needs drove them west
again. This time they were chased into the old
Roman walls of Chester, and, after a winter of starva-
tion, were hunted out of North Wales, and returned
through Northumbria to Mersea Island, in Essex.
But Mersea Island was insufficient to find food for
their numbers, and food was their chief necessity. In
the spring of 895 they sailed round the coast, and
towed their ships up the river Lea, to a place twenty

miles above London, where they made another burg, which has been identified with the earthworks of Walbury Camp, near Little Hallingbury. In the summer the Londoners tried to take the fort, but were put to flight. During harvest King Ælfred, being encamped near London to protect the harvesters, and one day riding up the river, noticed a place where the stream might be obstructed by building fortresses on either bank, and perhaps by stretching a chain or boom across the stream. He succeeded in "bottling" the ships, but the Danes rode off, once more across country. Their rapid rides are not surprising, for they commandeered the horses which were everywhere to be found (as in Iceland now-a-days, the usual means of transport), and rode them until they dropped. Reaching Quatford, below Bridgnorth, on the Severn, they built a fort—of which the mound remains—and wintered. But Wales would not receive them, and in the summer of 896 their host dispersed, some finding a refuge in Northumbria, others in East Anglia, and the greater part returning to France under Hástein, who soon afterwards settled on the land of Chartres, and became a great lord in the Frankish king's service.

So ended the great invasion. The Northumbrians and East Anglians still sent out war-vessels to the south coast, light "esks" of thirty or forty oars: in Icelandic the word *askar* is sometimes used in this sense, giving *askmenn*, the *ascmanni* of Adam of Bremen and *æscmen* of the Anglo-Saxons, signifying "pirates." King Ælfred designed larger ships to

,cope with these, but without much success. A small
engagement was won ; a fleet of twenty esks perished
on the south coast, and the attacks were abandoned. The century closed with the great king's
death, at peace with his former enemies.

And yet they were not all enemies who came to
England from the Northlands. We must not forget
"Ohthere, the old sea-captain, who dwelt in Halgo-
land," Ottar of the fjords north of Trondhjem, the
farmer and explorer, forerunner of Nansen as others of
his countrymen were of Nelson. Nor, again, must we
forget the voyage of Wulfstan (Ulfstein) to the eastern
shores of the Baltic, showing that even in this turbulent age peaceable travel and traffic were not only
possible, but the normal condition of things. We
read of battle and murder in the chronicles, as we
read in newspapers of salient events abroad, mostly
tragic ; but underlying all the tumult, land was tilled,
trade was pushed, and human life was lived in that
age as in our own.

Before Ælfred's death there were three distinct
states founded by the Danes, together forming
the Danelaw. It will make the story simpler if,
instead of carrying on the chronology of the whole
simultaneously, we take each in turn, beginning with
the district which was absorbed soonest into the
kingdom of Ælfred's family.

2. EAST ANGLIA.

The realm of Guthorm-Æthelstan included at first not only Norfolk and Suffolk, with Essex, which had recently been ruled by Kent as part of the eastern kingdom of the Saxons, but also the present counties of Cambridge, Huntingdon, Bedford, Buckingham, Hertford, and Middlesex. In 880 his army settled in the country conquered ten years earlier, and divided the lands. Their occupation of the western part of this large region did not last long, and the traces they left upon it, in place-names, racial character and customs are slight. In fact, they never settled it, in the sense of forming new estates to which the owners gave their names and national characteristics. They merely took possession, and that for a short tenure only. About 885, as already told, the boundary was refixed, and the whole of Middlesex and Buckingham-shire, with half Hertfordshire and Bedfordshire, were transferred to King Ælfred.

Guthorm-Æthelstan died in 890 or 891, and was succeeded by King Jórik (Eohric; that is to say, not *Eirik*, but a name formed like Jóstein). In 905 the peace of England was troubled by a cousin of King Eadward named Æthelwald, who had put in a claim to the throne, and now sought the help of the East Anglian Danes. They invaded Mercia, and Eadward made a counter raid into Cambridgeshire. The Danes returned, and caught the Kentish division of his army in their dilatory retreat. In the battle which followed the Danes held the field, but lost their king Jórik, Æthelwald the pretender, and "Ysopa" and Asketil the "holds"; *höldr* being a word which usually meant an owner of odal land, ancestral possessions, though in this case none of their holdings can have dated further back than twenty-five years.   No doubt it means here a large landowner ; the scale of precedence in Scandinavian society about this time was King, Jarl, Hersir (chief of a clan), Höld, Bóndi (yeoman), Leysingi (freedman), Thræll (slave).   As there was no clan-system among the immigrant Danes, who were adventurers under a leader, not tribes under a patriarch, the Höld in the East Anglian kingdom must have been next in rank to the Jarl.

Following this outburst, in 906 King Eadward made a treaty with the new king of East Anglia, Guthorm II., a son or nephew of Guthorm-Æthelstan.   Jórik, contrary to the terms of Wedmore, had been a pagan—at least Æthelwerd the chronicler tells us he " descended to Orcus," which implies as much,—and the new treaty provided that the Danes should abjure heathenism and respect church-sanctuary.   Something in the nature of international law was agreed upon ; offences were to be atoned by the English *wite* or the Danish *lah-slit* (*lag-slíð*) according as they were committed by one or the other nationality ; which indicates an intention on both sides to prevent border-raiding from becoming a *casus belli*.   In spite of this adoption of Christianity the bishopric of Elmham remained for some time in abeyance; but a little light is thrown on the conversion of the East Anglian Danes by the dedication of an early church at Norwich to St. Vedast, the Flemish saint whose name was probably introduced by Grimbald and his followers in King Ælfred's later years. There was also a church of St. Vedast in London, near St. Paul's, and another at Tathwell, in Lincolnshire, near Louth, which shows the range of the Flemish missionaries' enterprise. On the site of St. Vedast's at Norwich has been found an interesting monument—the shaft of a grave-cross carved with dragons in the style of Scandinavian art, and dated by Bishop Browne about 920. At Whissonsett (see an article by W. G. Collingwood, in *Trans. Norfolk Archæol. Soc.*, XV.), and at Cringleford, in Norfolk, are remains of other grave-crosses of a somewhat later type, showing influence from Mercia.

Trouble arose between Wessex and Northumbria, and East Anglia was drawn into it. In 913 King Eadward built a fort at Hertford on the north of the Lea. During May and June he marched upon Maldon in Essex, and built a burg at Witham; "a good part of the people, who were before under the dominion of the Danish men, submitted to him." The natives of Essex had not been exterminated; they were still Saxon, and easily became incorporated into the great Saxon kingdom; but now for the first time we find Scandinavians accepting—though for a time only—the rule of the king of Wessex. Jarl Thorketil and his hölds, "and almost all the chief men who owed obedience to Bedford, and also many of those who owed obedience to Northampton," sought him to be their lord. This was followed by the taking of Bedford and the fortification of Maldon in 917; after which, Thorketil and his men, troublesome subjects, were encouraged to emigrate, and went to France. Guthorm's kingdom was being carved away from him.

Shortly, however, there was a general rising of the East Anglian Danes. From Huntingdon they marched to Tempsford—not on the Thames, though the name preserves the saga-form of *Temps* as the name of the stream here crossed by a ford. At the junction of the Ivel and the Ouse they built a fort, similar perhaps to one described by Mr. A. R. Goddard (*Saga-book of the Viking Club*, iii. pp. 326-336). From this we gather that it was not unlike the entrenched camp containing a mound such as we have seen at Reading and Fulham, but more elaborate in its docks for boats like the *naust*, which can be seen at saga-sites in Iceland (see *Saga-steads of Iceland*, by Collingwood and Stefánsson). The only doubt in the identification is the elaborate nature of the fortress for a temporary purpose; but the Vikings were certainly skilful in military engineering, and probably requisitioned the labour from the surrounding farms and villages. Crossing the water they marched upon Bedford, but were met and overthrown by the townsfolk. It must be remembered that townsfolk in those days were not shopkeepers, but men on garrison-duty (see Maitland's *Domesday Book and Beyond*, p. 189). In recent years, skeletons, lying east and west, with swords and spearheads of the period, have been turned up in Russell Park, which must have been the battlefield. Then they attacked "Winganmere," from which they were repulsed. In the summer the whole army of Eadward took the fort at Tempsford, slaying King Guthorm II., "Toglea," and "Mannan"—Toli and Mani (Steenstrup, *Norm.* III., 51); and that autumn Colchester was besieged and stormed, with a general massacre of the inhabitants. In despair the last remnant of the Danish army, with the help of adventuring Vikings from abroad, beset Maldon, but were beaten off, and the conquest of East Anglia was achieved. King Eadward, having received the submission of jarl Thorfrith at Towcester, refortified Colchester, and the people of the whole kingdom once ruled by Guthorm-Æthelstan passed under the rule of Wessex.

For a while the government of the country was kept in the king's hands. King Æthelstan before his death (940) created out of East Anglia the first of the great ealdordoms, appointing to it Æthelstan of Devonshire, afterwards known as the "half-king." He retired into a monastery in 956, and his province was at first divided among his four sons; later, we find Æthelwold ruling East Anglia, succeeded, in 962, by his brother Æthelwine; in whose later years—he survived until 992—an acting governor was needed. The man was found in Ulfketil,[1] evidently a Dane by birth but English in his sympathies (see pp. 152, 153, 157).

In the ealdordom of East Anglia, Essex was not included. This county, with perhaps Middlesex,

[1] Ulfketil's name seems to be preserved in Ilketshall (*Ilketelshala* in *Domesday*), etc., near the "moated minster" not far from Bungay.—Note by the Rev. E. McClure.

Bucks., and Oxford, was assigned to Ælfgar, appointed later than Æthelstan the half-king. His son-in-law Brihtnoth succeeded him, and fell at Maldon in 991 ; followēd by Leofsige, who was banished 1002. And so the Danish kingdom gradually became a part of England ; leaving, however, many traces of its former independence.

One of the Suffolk hundreds took its name from the howe at which the Danish *Thing* was held, Thingoe or Tinghowe (Round's *Feudal England*, p. 98, quoting Gage's *Suffolk*, p. xii.). Abbot Sampson's survey (about 1185) gives the names of the twelve "leets" into which this hundred was divided, strictly according to the duodecimal system of the Scandinavians. Mr. Round compares the word "leet," of which he gives examples from *Domesday*, with the Danish *lægd*, or division of the county for military conscription, and we may add the nearer form of the Icelandic *leiˈð*, meaning at first a small local assembly, though ultimately the word was used for the third and last annual meeting of the Icelandic commonwealth. Near Buckingham is Tingewick, and in the south of Bedfordshire is Tingrith (Tingrye in 1250). But East Anglia is not divided into trithings and wapentakes, as were parts which the Danes not only ruled but settled : even Northamptonshire was not assessed at Domesday by carucates but by hides, like Wessex ; only the hides, Mr. Round finds, were taken in groups of fours, just as the Mercian shilling contained four pence ; while Cambridgeshire is assessed for the most part in terms of five hides, on the non-Danish system.

At the same time there are plentiful traces of Danish occupation, even in Cambridgeshire. The parish names of Toftes and Quoy (Coeia in *Domesday* = *Kví*, = quey or quoy in Orkney and Shetland, a fold, used in Kvíá and Kvíabekkr in Iceland); Burwell Nest or Ness, a point of land reaching out into the fens; Denney, here perhaps representing *Dana-ey*, the Danes' island in the fens; Duxford or Dokesworth, from Toki, a Dane; "Daneland towards Holgate weye," mentioned *temp.* Edward III. as in Haslingfield; the Danes' Bottom—compare the common use of *botn* in Iceland, in Cumberland and in Cleveland for the *head* of a valley (as opposed to its ordinary English use for the *basin* of a valley),—these names are given by Mr. Hailstone in a paper read to the Viking Club (*Saga-book*, iv., pp. 108–126). He mentions also that certain lands are noted in Domesday as paying two *ores* as toll, showing that the Scandinavian money-system still obtained there; that the priest Herolf, a Scandinavian name, was appointed by Æthelstan head of the monastic house at Biggin Abbey; that under Eadward the Confessor one "Turcus" (Thorgest?) held land in Reach and Burwell under Ramsey Abbey; and that in Ditton Camoys, Westley and Sixmile Bottom a six-hide reckoning prevailed. Later, though these Scandinavian owners may have come in with Knút, we find mentioned in *Domesday* Anschetil, Thurstan, Tochi, Torchil and Turkell; in the *Inquisitio Eliensis* Grim, Omund, Osketil, Oslac and Simund; and in *Feet of Fines*, Aki, as holding lands in the county of Cambridge.

The Danes of East Anglia, however, seem to have

congregated into the towns, in Colchester, Bedford, Huntingdon and Cambridge; and though the ten wards of Cambridge did not correspond with the Scandinavian reckoning by six and twelve, the fact that each of the wards was under a "lawman" points to a prevalence of Danish tradition in the eleventh century. The great colony of "byes" clusters round Yarmouth, though there are two Wilbys, Colby and Risby inland, and Kirby in Essex. Thwaite, near Bungay, is a Scandinavian name of Norse type; and place-names ending in -hoe, -well, -wall (-vellir) and -stead may be Danish. The word "staithe," common along the east coast, represents the Icelandic *stöð* in the sense of "harbour": and "carr," representing Icel. *kjarr*, is used for land once covered with copse. On the coast the names in -wich, -haven, and -ness or Naze have a Northern origin: but though these traces of Danish occupation can be found, especially on the seaboard of the districts, they are by no means so noticeable as in the rest of the Danelaw, where Viking occupation was of longer endurance.

3. THE FIVE BOROUGHS:

Nottingham, Leicester, Derby, Stamford and Lincoln.

When Halfdan's vikings, in 877, overran Mercia for the third time they left the south-western half of it to Ceolwulf, who had been tributary king of the whole since 874. Ælfred gained this territory in 885

or 886, and set over it his son-in-law Æthelred, who
held it until 912 ; after which his widow Æthelflæd,
the Lady of the Mercians, ruled it.   At her death, in
919, King Eadward took the province into his own
hands.

The north-eastern part of Mercia was divided in
877 among such of Halfdan's veterans as had not
received land in Northumbria the year before.   This
district, though at first under Halfdan's influence, was
not previously, and later on ceased to be, a part of
the Northumbrian realm.   After the treaty between
Ælfred and Guthorm-Æthelstan, its southernmost part
was north of Stony Stratford, where the East Anglian
and Saxon boundaries met on Watling Street.   In its
widest extent it must have included the present counties of Nottingham, Leicester, Derby, Rutland and
Lincoln, with the greater part of Northamptonshire
and parts of Stafford and Cheshire.

But as Mr. Round has shown, not even all this
district was in the full sense settled by the Danes
(*Feudal England*, p. 69).   Their land-measurement,
by carucates, applies in *Domesday* to Nottingham,
Leicester, Derby, Rutland and Lincoln, but not to
the rest of the territory : there is even a difference
between Leicestershire and the more thoroughly
Danish districts, for its lands are not reckoned in
hundreds of twelve carucates, although Leicester itself
was a thoroughly Danish town.   On the other hand,
part of Warwickshire had some Danish colonies, such
as Rugby, which is south-west of Watling Street.   In a
word, the Danes did not care to spread themselves

too loosely over a hostile country : they grouped themselves round the great strongholds which formed the bases of their organisation.

These great strongholds were the Five Burgs or Boroughs : Lincoln, once a Roman colony at the junction of the Fosse Way with Ermine Street ; Stamford, where Ermine Street crossed the Welland ; Leicester, where the Fosse Way crossed the Soar ; Derby, where Ryknield Street crossed the Derwent ; and Nottingham, where another old route going north and south crossed the Trent. Of these, Derby was practically a Danish creation ; as Northweorthig, it had been only a small Anglian village ; now it grew to importance as Deoraby. Lindsey and Leicester had been bishops' sees ; that of Leicester was removed to Dorchester, and that of Lindsey disappeared for over eighty years.

Each of the five boroughs seems to have been under a jarl of its own, with its own military organisation. Internal affairs, in the case of Stamford and Lincoln, were managed by twelve "lawmen," and probably the same arrangement was followed in the other towns. When Chester grew to some importance through trade with Ireland, it also had its "lawmen," and the Lagmen of the Islands are mentioned in the tenth century as leaders of invasion in Ireland ; the chief justice of Orkney was called "lagman." The title seems to have meant much the same as the "Law-speaker" of the Icelandic Althing, that is to say, chief of a court, who knew the law and stated it ; the existence of twelve such men seem to imply twelve wards in each town of which the lagmen were the presidents.

Another characteristic of the Danish districts is the use of the "long hundred," 120 for 100. The houses in the town and the acres in the county of Lincoln are so reckoned in *Domesday*, and the survival of this notation to modern times is seen even in *Whitaker's Almanac*, which tells us that in the timber trade 120 deals = 100, and that on the East coast fish are still counted by the long hundred (in this case = 132). "Six score to the hundred" is still familiar to Lake District gardeners and wood-mongers. Twelve carucates made a territorial hundred, and twelve marks a monetary hundred, in the Danish part of England, just as the word *hundraδ* in old Icelandic always meant 120 ; for example, when the saga says that the bodyguard of King Olaf numbered a "hundred" men, sixty huskarls and sixty "guests."

In Leicestershire, which was less completely Danish than Lincolnshire, the land was not reckoned in hundreds of twelve carucates, though it was a carucated district : the hide of Leicestershire was a sum of eighteen carucates (Round, *Feudal England*, p. 82). This is borne out by the ancient place-names as seen in the Leicestershire Survey (1124–1129), in which the proportion of obviously Scandinavian origin is not very great; out of 174 entries there are 38 "byes," and a few such as Thormodeston, Thurketleston, Grimeston, Ravenston and Normanton, betraying the name of a Danish settler, with Tunga and Houwes, making a little more than a quarter of the whole. In Lincolnshire, on the other hand, though " even in this country, taken as a whole, it would be difficult to say whether the names of Norse or English origin predominate," yet " let the eye run over a map from Theddlethorpe, on the coast, through Withern, Ruckland, Scamblesby, Thimbleby, Coningsby, Revesby, Firsby, to Skegness, and it will be found that names, other than Danish, in this large area may be almost counted on the fingers " (*Lincolnshire and the Danes*, by the Rev. G. S. Streatfeild, pp. 10, 16). Mr. Streatfeild notes that the map shows three main streams of Danish immigration ; one from Burton Stather up the valley of the Trent and towards Lincoln and Caistor ; another from Grimsby and a third from Skegness spreading inland, but leaving some spaces between these groups to the old Anglian inhabitants, and generally avoiding the Fen district, though there was a colony between Boston and the coast, and west of the fens South Kesteven is filled with " byes " suburban to Stamford. " Nowhere near Boston is there a *by* or a *thorpe* (unless we except Fenthorpe). If we may venture upon an inference from this peculiarity, it is that the Northmen who settled at Brothertoft, Pinchbeck, Wigtoft (Wiketoft, once on the coast), and other parts of the fen, did so at a later period." The settlement at first was not a clearance of the English : in many cases it was merely a change of owners ; but gradually the Danes increased in numbers, either from the natural growth of population, or from additional immigrations, or both, and new land was taken up.

Hence we find, around such pre-Viking names as
Alford, Horncastle, Partney, Tetford, Belchford and
Donington in the south wolds, and Frodingham, Bottes-
ford, Caistor, Glanford Brigg, Binbrook and Ludford
in the north, groups of Danish place-names, chiefly
"byes," showing that individuals took up land on the
wolds, till then uncultivated. "Thorpes," indicating
villages as opposed to "byes" or isolated farmsteads, and either Scandinavian or Anglian in origin
are found more plentifully on the lower and richer
pastures, where the earlier settlers had their estates
which were worked by the natives. Though the
Danes certainly owned thralls, it is not a little
remarkable that in later years the proportion of freemen to slaves was much greater in the Danelaw than
in the rest of England, and greatest of all in the most
Danish districts and in the manors of Danish origin.
Professor Maitland (*Domesday Book and Beyond*, p. 22)
noted that at the time of Domesday the number
of *servi* was at its maximum in Cornwall and
Gloucestershire, very low in Norfolk, Suffolk, Derby,
Leicester, Middlesex and Sussex, but *nil* in Yorkshire
and Lincolnshire. The number of sokemen (or
comparatively free men, owing certain dues to the
Hundred courts or to a lord, but otherwise masters
of their own land, somewhat like the customary
tenants of Cumberland) was greater in Norfolk and
Suffolk than in Essex, while in Lincolnshire they
formed nearly half the rural population. In William
the Conqueror's time there were in Lincolnshire
11,503 sokemen, 7,723 villans, and 4,024 bordars ; in

Yorkshire only 447 sokemen against 5,079 villans and
1,819 bordars, but this was after the ravaging of
Yorkshire when the free population either perished or
was brought into an inferior position, while Lincolnshire escaped with less damage, and showed the old
state of society as in King Eadward's days.   At
Domesday time there were few sokemen left in
Cambridgeshire, Bedfordshire, Herts. and Bucks.,
but they were thick in Leicestershire, Notts. and
Northamptonshire.   K. Rhamm, quoted by Prof.
Vinogradoff (*Eng. Hist. Rev.*, xxi., p. 357), seems
in a recent work to regard sokemen as a Danish
alternative for villans, and developed out of leysings
or freedmen.   As they existed also in Kent, they
must not be supposed a specially Scandinavian
institution, but they were more plentiful, not only in
Danish as compared with English districts, but in
Danish as compared with English manors.   In
Lincolnshire, counting the sokemen, villans and
bordars of the Survey, it is found that in the manors
with distinctively English names the sokemen
numbered two-fifths of the population, while in
manors with names suggesting Danish origin they
formed three-fifths (Boyle, *Hull Literary Club*, 1895).
We may perhaps say that in the Danelaw they
represent the original freeholders of the settlement,
who even as odal proprietors owed at least obedience
to the local *Thing*, from which the transition to their
place in Anglo-Saxon England was easy.   It was in
the districts not forcibly conquered by King Eadward
the Elder that the free settlers remained and flourished,

and their tendency, whether from racial instinct or from the influence of Christianity newly adopted, was toward personal liberty, the independence of peasant proprietors and of travelling traders.

Of trade with Scandinavia in this earlier part of the tenth century we can only infer from the sagas that it was possible. In Egil's saga we find Thórólf Kveldúlfsson (d. about 877) sending a ship from Norway with dried fish, tallow, hides and furs to England, where "they found a good market, loaded the ship with wheat, honey, wine and cloth, and sailed back in the autumn to Hordaland." But the trade of Björn the Chapman, Harald Fairhair's son, from Túnsberg in South Norway to Denmark and Germany, did not seem to reach England directly; few English coins of the earlier part of the tenth century have been found in Norway and Sweden, fewer still in Denmark. Commerce from the Danelaw at this time must have begun with Flanders and Frisia, and gradually extended its range. Torksey seems to have taken the lead as a mercantile centre; Nottingham followed, and in less than a century had a merchant-gild.

The increasing wealth and comfort of life, as well as the adoption of Christianity, is shown by the monuments. In Lincolnshire, at Crowle, Bassingham and Edenham, there are fragments of stone carving which may be assigned to the tenth century; in Northamptonshire, at Mears Ashby; in Staffordshire at Checkley, Leek (the cross-bearer), Alstonefield (the warrior shaft), and Rolleston; in Derbyshire, at Norbury and Hope, and at St. Alkmund's, Derby, where the dragon-

design is as Scandinavian as that of St. Vedast's at
Norwich. These examples, to which more might be
added, shows how the settlers began to assimilate
themselves to the culture they found in England :
and as art goes hand-in-hand with manufacture and
trade, we may assume that the life of the settlers was
not all fighting and farming, when they came through
the initial period of trouble which we have now to
review.

Chester, though the ruins of the Roman station had
been seized and held by Hástein, was a place of no
importance at the beginning of the tenth century. The
Irish trade had not arisen ; White and Black Gaill
were still disputing Dublin, and the Danes of Mercia
did not see, as ealdorman Æthelred did, the value of
the position.   In 907 or 908 he repaired the fortifications and created the town, perhaps at that time
introducing the priory of St. Werburgh, a Mercian
dedication.   This was the first step toward the great
work he undertook of strengthening English Mercia
against further encroachment, and of capturing the
land of the Five Boroughs.

The forward policy of Mercia developed into war.
There was fighting on both sides of Watling Street.
The Saxons raided over the border for five weeks ;
the Danes fought them at Tettenhall near Wolverhampton, and were beaten.   Eadward went south to
fit out a fleet against the east coast, and the Danes
raided the Severn Valley, returning by way of Quatford
near Bridgnorth, where Hástein's men had wintered,
and at Wednesfield another great victory was won by

the Saxons; in which two kings, two jarls and other leading men were slain. When ealdorman Æthelred died, his widow Æthelflæd, the Lady of the Mercians, continued his policy of building forts to protect English Mercia, and the war against East Anglia naturally drew the Five Boroughs more and more into conflict with the growing Anglo-Saxon power.

On St. John the Baptist's day of 918 (Florence of Worcester), the Northampton and Leicester Danes attacked the fort at Towcester, and, failing to storm it, raided Buckinghamshire. But when Colchester was taken and the kingdom of East Anglia came to an end, the resistance of the Five Boroughs weakened. Early in 919 Leicester made voluntary submission to the Lady of the Mercians, and even York offered adherence to her. In April King Eadward marched to Stamford, built a fort on the south bank of the Welland, and received the submission of the neighbourhood. Thence he went to Nottingham, which had been captured by his troops; he repaired the fortifications "and stationed both English and Danes therein."

This is the beginning of a new policy. The king of Wessex became actual and personal lord of a mixed population of Angles and Danes. It was no longer a question of mutual slaughter, but of a *modus vivendi*; the Danes were already there, and after thirty years' possession they had taken root in the soil. But as the earlier part of this war had been a war of extermination, driving the Danes from the southern counties, the change in attitude is noteworthy. The southern counties were Saxon, and must be cleared of the intruders ; in these Anglian districts all were aliens to Wessex, and there was no question of driving out the Danes if they would live peaceably and own Eadward's rule.

He was now master of four out of the Five Boroughs. His sister, the Lady of the Mercians, was dead, and he took her province into his own hands, carrying out her work. In 920 he built a fort at "Manchester in Northumbria," and in 921 another at Bakewell in Derbyshire, where (as the Winchester Chronicle asserts) he received the adhesion of all the rulers of the north, except those of the Orkneys and Hebrides. It is not stated that they appeared before him in person and gave their kingdoms into his hands; "they chose him for father and for lord." It was before the days of feudalism, though this was twisted by mediæval lawyers into the performance of feudal homage with all it involved. The northern states saw that he was the dominant power, gradually advancing toward them, and they hastened to forestall his attack and to court his assistance. With Ragnvald of York and "all those who dwelt in Northumbria, as well English as Danes and Northmen and others," the jarl of Lincoln must have come in or sent his envoys, if he had not done so earlier. There is no word of fighting in Lincolnshire, but the independence of the Five Boroughs was now a thing of the past.

4. THE KINGDOM OF YORK.

Ivar and Halfdan captured York on November 1, 867, and next year set out for further conquests in the south, leaving the kingdom of Northumbria—that is to say Deira, or the part of Northumbria south of Tyne —under an Englishman, Ecgberht. The *Libellus de Rebus Saxonicis*, an early authority, gives him a reign of five years, succeeded by Richsi for two years, and names Ecgberht as king for two years more. Symeon of Durham makes Ricsig king in 877 (*Letter on the Archbishops of York*); Mr. J. R. Green identifies him with Bagsecg; others regard him as a native tributary king of Bernicia. It was not until 875 that Halfdan returned from the campaign against Ælfred, and next year dealt out the lands of Northumbria to his followers.

The southern limit of Northumbria was much the same as that of modern Yorkshire and Lancashire; we have seen that it included Manchester. The northern limit was still the Tyne, beyond which, though Halfdan penetrated in 876, he did not person- ally rule, for the government was left in the hands of Ecgberht, probably the Englishman who had ruled Northumbria as tributary king, and now founded the long line of ealdormen or high-reeves of Bernicia with head-quarters at Bamborough. The Danes did not settle in Bernicia; even in county Durham their place- names are comparatively rare, although this is no absolute test of their presence or absence. Where

the land was already filled with population, and not so
completely ravaged as to need fresh colonisation, the
new owners simply carried on the "going concern"
under the old name : in many parts, however, we find
groups of Scandinavian place-names so close and thick
that we must assume either depopulation by war or
the nearly complete absence of previous population.
There is no reason to suppose that the earlier Vikings
depopulated the country they ravaged ; they came for
spoil, and the slaughter was an incident. Canon
Atkinson has shown, by his analysis of the area in
Cleveland under cultivation at Domesday time, that
very little of the countryside in that district was other
than forest or moor even at the end of the eleventh
century, and that most of the villages then existing
had Scandinavian names. His conclusion is that
Cleveland was a wilderness, first penetrated (since
prehistoric and Roman days) by the Danes and
Norse, except for a few clearings such as Crathorne,
Stokesley, Stainton and Easington, besides the old
monastery at Whitby.

This conclusion receives curious support from an
analysis of the sculptured stones now to be seen at
old churchyard sites in Cleveland.   It is only at
Yarm, Crathorne, Stainton, Easington, and Whitby
that we find monuments of the pre-Viking age, and
these are products of the latest Anglian period ; at
Osmotherley, Ingleby Arncliffe, Welbury, Kirkleving-
ton, Thornaby, Ormesby, Skelton, Great Ayton,
Kirkdale and Kirkby-in-Cleveland are tombstones of
the tenth and eleventh centuries.   It is obvious that

the Angles were only beginning to penetrate Cleveland
when the Vikings invaded and carried on the work
of land-settlement much further. Subsequently, we
shall see (p. 178) further extension was made by Norse
from the west coast, as place-names show; but the
place-names alone are far from trustworthy as in-
dications of settlement. An analysis of the monuments shows that in many cases pre-Viking art-work
exists at places with Scandinavian names (*e.g.* Kirkby
Moorside, Kirkby Misperton, Kirkdale), while in other
cases only Viking Age crosses are found at places
with names presumably Anglian (*e.g.* Ellerburn,
Levisham, Sinnington, Nunnington). The inference
is that, in the east of Yorkshire especially, some
Anglian sites were depopulated and refounded with
Danish names, while others had no importance in
Anglian times, but soon became flourishing sites under
the Danes. In the west of Yorkshire the great dales
were already tenanted by the Angles, but the moors
between them, and the sites high up the valleys, were
not sites of churches until the Danish period (see
further in "Anglian and Anglo-Danish Sculpture in
the North Riding," by W. G. Collingwood, *Yorks.
Arch. Journ.*, 1907).

Yorkshire at Domesday was carucated, and divided
into Ridings (trithings) and Wapentakes. Thingwall
near Whitby (Canon Atkinson, site lost), Thinghow, near
Guisborough (now lost), and Thinghou, now Finney
Hill, near Northallerton (Mr. William Brown, F.S.A.),
Tingley near Wakefield, Thingwall near Liverpool,
Thingwall in Wirral, may have been Thingsteads. It

has been suggested by the Rev. E. Maule Cole that
Wetwang in the East Riding was once a "place of
summons" for some crime committed there, preserving
the Icelandic word *vætt-vangr*. Sites named "Lund"
possibly indicate sacred groves : there are such in
Holderness, near Beverley, near Selby, in Amounderness, in Furness, between Dent and Sedbergh, and
near Appleby in Westmorland : here, perhaps, early
settlers, like Thórir at Lund in Iceland, " worshipped
the grove" (*Landnáma*, iii. 17). But the names
in -ergh and -ark, by writers of the past generation
supposed to mean *hörgr*, "a shrine," are simply dairy-
farms—*erg*, i.e. *setr*, as *Orkn. Saga* explains, and as
Dr. Colley March has shown conclusively.

North Lancashire was part of Craven, and carucated.
South Lancashire in *Domesday* had six hundreds, and
both carucates and hides are mentioned.   Professor
Maitland thought (*Domesday Book and Beyond*, p. 470)
that the hides were recent.   But Lancashire in Halfdan's day was merely an unimportant part of Deira ;
its broad mosslands were not taken up until the
coming of the Norse in 900 (p. 191).   Cumberland and
Westmorland also were little colonised by the Danes ;
a few relics show immigration at this early age by the
Stainmoor route, but the Danes at first do not seem
to have ventured to settle far from their town centres,
and the wilder scenery and rougher Celtic population
of the west had no attractions for them.   Symeon of
Durham (*sub anno* 1092) notes that the city of Carlisle
had remained uninhabited for 200 years after its
destruction by the Danes, until William Rufus re-

founded it.   Halfdan's colony was mainly confined to
Yorkshire.

One interesting episode of the period tends to con-
firm this conclusion.   On Halfdan's raid into Bernicia
(875) Eardwulf, abbot of Lindisfarne, fled before the
storm, carrying with him the relics of St. Cuthbert,
and wandered from refuge to refuge for nine years ;
so Symeon says, though probably the period was much
shorter.   His journeyings throw some light on the
state of the country at the time, and they can be
partly traced from the traditions given by Symeon and
Reginald of Durham, and from early dedications of
churches near which there is some presumption that
the relics rested in their wandering.   The guide of
the party was abbot Eadred " Lulisc," of Caer-Luel or
Carlisle, whose monastery must have been destroyed
about the same time.   The earlier part of the
route has been traced by Monsignor Eyre, and the
later by the late Rev. T. Lees, from ancient dedications to St. Cuthbert, which, taken for what they are
worth, suggest that the fugitives went at first inland to
Elsdon, then by the Reed and Tyne to Haydon
Bridge and up the South Tyne Valley, south by the
Maiden Way, and so through the fells, by Lorton and
Embleton, to the Cumberland coast.   At Derwent
Mouth (Workington) they determined to embark for
Ireland, but were driven back by a storm and thrown
upon the coast of Galloway, where they found a refuge
at Whithorn, which (see further on p. 225) may have
already been occupied by the Viking colony of Gallgael.
In this storm the MS. *Gospels* of bishop Eadfrith

(now in the British Museum) was washed overboard, but recovered. At Whithorn the bishop heard news of Halfdan's death, and turned homewards by way of Kirkcudbright. Now the fact that the relics of St. Cuthbert found refuge in Cumberland and Galloway shows that the Danish invasion from which they were saved took very little hold of these parts. The Vikings of the Irish Sea were already, if not Christianised, at least under the influence of Christians, and not hostile to the fugitive monks, while the natives welcomed them.

The date and circumstances of Halfdan's death are not easily set down. The *Libellus* above quoted does not place him on the list of Northumbrian kings. The *Annals of Ulster* mention under 876, *recte* 877, " Alband," king of the Dubhgaill, killed in a battle on Strangford Lough with the Finngaill. The tenth-century History of St. Cuthbert, which calls him and his brother *Scaldingi*, Skjöldungs, says that in the end he became mad and unpopular with his army, which expelled him ; Symeon of Durham adds that he fled with three ships from the Tyne, and shortly perished. These authors then tell the curious story of the election of Guthred, his successor. Eadred, abbot of Carlisle, who was with St. Cuthbert's relics at Craik in central Yorkshire on the way home, dreamt that St. Cuthbert told him to go to the Danish army on the Tyne, and to ransom from slavery a boy named Guthred, son of Hardecnut (John of Wallingford says that "the sons of Hardecnut had sold him into slavery "), and present him to the army as their king.

He was also to ask the army to give him the land between Tyne and Wear, as a gift to St. Cuthbert and a sanctuary for criminals. Confident in his mission, he carried out its directions, found the boy, ransomed him, gained the army's consent and the gift of the land, and proclaimed Guthred king at "Oswigedune." Eardwulf then brought to the same place the relics of St. Cuthbert, on which every one swore good faith and "lived happily ever after." The relics remained until 999 at Chester-le-Street, and there Eardwulf re-established the bishopric.

The date of Guthred's election is given by Symeon as 883, but if he reigned (as the *Libellus* says) for fourteen years, it must have occurred a little earlier; in fact in 880, not long after the death of Halfdan, if he were the king slain at Strangford Lough. Though there is so much legend attached to Guthred's name, his subsequent history shows that he was a peaceful and Christian king, curiously illustrating the rapidity with which Viking colonists, if not treated as enemies, became "acclimatised." Until nearly the end of his reign he never came into collision with Wessex: he swore peace with Ælfred at the coming of Hástein; and Æthelnoth, ealdorman of Somerset, is said by Æthelwerd to have made York the base of his operations against Hástein. This new attitude of the Danish colony is shown by the statement that Sigeferth (Sigfrith jarl from Dublin?) landed twice, and ravaged the Northumbrian coast, after the taking of Benfleet during Hástein's invasion: Vikings turned bourgeois were fair game.

Guthred's kingdom was indeed to some extent Christian. The bishopric of Lindisfarne, threatneed at first, was even brought nearer to the Danish colony by the transference of the see to Chester-le-Street : the archbishopric of York survived the upheaval, and Wulfhere, its archbishop, died, in 892, having escaped the invasion in his retreat at Addingham in Wharfedale (Symeon). Guthred, dying on St. Bartholomew's day, Aug. 24, 894, was buried in the high church at York.

During four years there was, Æthelwerd notes, great discord, "because of the foul bands of Danes who still remained throughout Northumberland": meaning that there was an unsettled state of affairs. The bishopric at Chester-le-Street continued, Eardwulf being succeeded, in 899 or 900, by Cutheard ; but it was not until 900 or 901 that Æthelbald was consecrated archbishop of York. In 901 Æthelwald the pretender, who was killed (p. 101) together with King Jórik of East Anglia, went to Northumbria to seek help which should put him on the throne of Wessex. He was elected king of York, and so Northumbria received another Christian ruler, one of the West Saxon royal family, though hostile to the reigning king of Wessex. At his death, in 905, the Northumbrians made peace with King Eadward : and we have no further notices of their choice of a ruler until 911, when we find Ecwils (or Eowils, Jógísl?) and Halfdan as joint kings, or kings of a divided realm. Florence of Worcester, after naming them, injudiciously interpolates "brothers of king Hinguar" : but as Halfdan the brother of Ivar had been fighting

at the head of the army which came to England in
866 and had disappeared since 876, this must have
been a second king Halfdan.

These kings were drawn into the war between
Eadward and East Anglia ; they invaded Mercia, and
fell at Wednesfield near Wolverhampton with the jarls
Ottar and Scrufa (Skrúf-hárr, " curly haired "?), the
hölds Othulf, Benesing, Thurferth, Guthferth and
Agmund, Osferth the "collector" (or the Little; Steenstrup, *Norm.* III., 35), Anlaf the Black and Guthferth.

In 919 York submitted to the Lady of the Mercians,
and for the moment it seemed· that the independence
of the Danish kingdom was at an end.   But in May
she died, and soon afterwards " Inguald " (according
to Symeon) took York, meaning Ragnvald, Reignold,
Ronald, Ranald, Reginald—according to the various
adaptations of his name—one of the most romantic
figures of Viking story.   Ragnvald mac Bicloch of the
family of Ivar had ravaged Dunblane in 912, slain
Bard Ottarsson off the Isle of Man in 914, and in 915
joined the Vikings at Waterford with his brother or
cousin Sigtrygg Gale O'Ivar, who became king of
Dublin in 916.   Then joining jarl Ottar, who had
been concerned in the unfortunate attack on South
Wales and Herefordshire in 915, and had been nearly
starved to death on Flatholme or Steepholme in the
Bristol Channel, Ragnvald set out for adventure in
North Britain.   He probably landed in Cumberland,
crossed country by the Roman Wall, and fought the
battle of which we have soon to ·hear.   In 919
Ragnvald became king of York, the first of the series

of Irish Viking rulers who were not finally expelled until 954.

Bernicia, equivalent to the modern county of Northumberland with the Lothians, a purely English territory from the Tyne to the Forth, was then under the rule of Ealdred and his brother Uhtred, sons of Eadulf, lord of Bamborough and ealdorman of Bernicia, King Ælfred's friend, who died in 912. He was the son of Ecgberht, who had been the tributary king of Northumbria under Halfdan, and in 875 had apparently been deputed to govern the northern part of the realm in which Halfdan's Danes never settled. The brothers Ealdred and Uhtred, Eadulf's sons, kept up their friendly relations with Eadward of Wessex, and appear among those who chose him for father and lord in 921, though in this sudden invasion of the Irish vikings the friendship of Wessex was of no avail.

There are two curious stories given side by side in the tenth-century History of St. Cuthbert, which, taken together with the Ulster Annals and the Pictish Chronicle, throw some little light on the times. The first story is that Elfred, son of Birihtulfing (of the family of Brihtwulf), fleeing from pirates, came over the western hills (i.e. from Cumberland, now being settled by the Norse) and bishop Cutheard gave him certain vills, which can be recognised as the eastern part of county Durham. At last Ragnvald came to the land of Aldred Eadulf's son, who got help from Constantine of Scotland, and fought Ragnvald at Corbridge, but was defeated. Elfred was slain, but Aldred and his brother Uhtred escaped. The other story is that Edred, son

of Rixinc (Richsi-ing, descendant of Richsi or Ricsig),
rode west over the hills (to Cumberland), and there
killed the prince Eardulf and carried off his wife. He
took sanctuary with Cutheard, who gave him the eastern
part of county Durham, bounded by Deor street (the
Roman road), and also the land of Gainford-on-Tees,
which he held three years, until Ragnvald slew him
at the battle of Corbridge, and gave the land to Esbrid,
son of Edred, and his brother Eltan the jarl, for their
services in the battle.   In these stories we have hints
of affairs and persons in Cumberland, not without
value considering the darkness of the period ; and
we are assured of the persistence of St. Cuthbert's
patrimony in county Durham as a sanctuary, in spite
of all the attacks of the Vikings.   This is enforced by
the legend of Olaf Ball (*ballr*, the stubborn) to whom
Ragnvald had given the land from Castle Eden to the
Wear, a pagan who refused rent and service to St.
Cuthbert.   Coming in one day to the church at
Chester-le-Street, he shouted to bishop Cutheard and
his congregation, " What can your dead man, Cuthbert, do to me ?   What is the use of threatening me
with his anger?   I swear, by my strong gods Thor
and Othan, that I will be the enemy of you all from
this time forth."   And when he tried to leave the
church he could not lift his foot over the threshold,
but fell down dead, "and St. Cuthbert, as was just, got
his lands."

Now the Ulster Annals, under 918, describe a
battle in which King Ragnvald with Gotfrith O'Ivar
and the jarls Ottar and "Gragabai" met the men of

I

Alban and the northern Saxons, and fought a battle
in which the Scots were victorious at first but were
routed by Ragnvald's ambush; the same tactics he
had used just before to decide a battle in Ireland.
The Pictish Chronicle tells that Constantine in his
eighteenth year (918) fought Ragnvald at Tinemore
(Tynemoor, near Corbridge) and the Scots were
victorious. The fact remains that next year Ragnvald
took York.

Ragnvald O'Ivar, king of White and Black Gaill—
of his own Norse and the Danes of Northumbria—
died in 921 (*Annals of Ulster*). If 921 is the year
of the submission of the North at Bakewell, the
chronological difficulty about Ragnvald's part in it
vanishes. In the same year Guthfrith O'Ivar took
Dublin, driving out Sigtrygg Gale O'Ivar, who
thereupon took Ragnvald's place at York. In 925
he went to Tamworth on a visit, was baptised, and
married Æthelstan's sister.

Æthelstan was now pushing his influence still
farther north than his father Eadward had reached.
In 926 he met Constantine, king of Scots, Owain, king
of Cumbria (the land from Derwentwater to Dumbarton) and Ealdred of Bamborough at Dacor, probably
Dacre in Cumberland on the borders of territory in
the Strathclyde and Scottish power. It may be that
a young son of the Scottish king was baptised on the
occasion; the tie of "compaternity" with Æthelstan
was worth obtaining. It may also be that the northern kings promised to renounce — if not "idol-
atry"—their alliance with heathens. Constantine's

kingdom was a small one, the eastern part of Scotland from the Forth to the Moray Firth, and he was hard pressed on all sides by the Vikings of Orkney, the Hebrides, Galloway, and Northumbria. It was an error on the part of thirteenth-century lawyers to construe this into feudal homage ; and the Saxon chroniclers no doubt overstated the significance of the meeting. But it showed that Æthelstan was soon to be master of England, though the Cumbrian and Scottish kings could not keep their pledges of alliance.

Sigtrygg O'Ivar, " king of Black and White Gaill," died in 927 (Ulster Annals rectified). By a. former wife he left sons, Guthfrith, Harald and Olaf Cuaran ; " Sithfrey and Oisley " (Sigfrith and Háisl) are also mentioned as Sigtrygg's sons, killed at Brunanburh. Guthfrith, trying to succeed his father at York, was expelled by Æthelstan, and took refuge with the Scots ; so did Olaf, who became son-in-law to King Constantine. The countenance given to the Viking chiefs was regarded by Æthelstan as a *casus belli*. In 934 he led his army into Strathclyde, put to flight Owain of Cumbria and marched through Constantine's country to " Wertermor and Dunfoeder " (identified by Skene with Kirriemuir and Dunnotar, near Stonehaven), while his fleet ravaged the coast as far as the Norse settlement of Caithness.

Brunanburh (937) was the " return match." Such an invasion called for revenge, and Constantine organised revenge on a grand scale. Three chief powers joined their arms—the Scots, the Cumbrians, and the Vikings of the West. The Orkney and

Northumberland states do not appear to have shared
in the confederacy, though Æthelstan, ten years
before, had expelled Ealdred from Bamborough, but
apparently reinstated him. The expedition, if this
battle were fought on the north-east coast of England,
would have passed the Orkneys, and met with either
help or hindrance ; and the land forces of Scots and
Cumbrians—for they surely would not embark and
disembark when the roads which Æthelred had used
would serve them as well—must have marched south,
either by the east coast or the west : if the former,
they would have met with resistance or adherence in
Bernicia and at York, but of all this we hear nothing.
If, however, they came by Cumbria and along the
Maiden Way, they could penetrate far south without
touching the more populous and settled districts
under English rule. The fleet, numbering 615 ships,
an enormous number to pilot on a long voyage, came
from the Hebrides, Dublin, Limerick and Waterford,
that is to say from all the Viking ports in the west.
This we gather from the *Annals of Clonmacnois*, which
mention Geleachan, king of the Islands (Sudreyjar) ;
Moylemurry, son of Cossewarra (or Cossa-uara), named
as a chief at Waterford in 916 ; Arick mac Brith, *i.e.*
Hàrek Bard's son, connected with Limerick by his
brother Colla, lord of that town in 924, and with
Irish royalties by another brother who married the
daughter of Domhnall, son of King Aedh Finnliath.
The object of this expedition was to strike at Æthelstan
as he had struck at Scotland. The natural meeting-
point of all these various confederates was somewhere

about the Mersey or the Dee. It is true that Florence of Worcester names the Humber as the estuary entered by the fleet, but it is hardly conceivable that 615 ships should have been taken all round by Pentland Firth or Land's End when any of the estuaries on the west coast would serve as a port, and a landing in any one of them would further the objects of the expedition better than the desolation of the Danclaw. After Vínheidi (perhaps Brunanburh, as described in Egil's Saga), one Alfgeir rode in flight night and day to "Jarlsnes," the Earl's Ness, mentioned also in *Orkneyinga Saga* (chap. 72) as in Bretland (Wales), for which Mr. A. G. Moffat suggests a site near Swansea. This, so far as it has any weight, adds to the probability of the western site for Brunanburh.

The various names of the battle-fields are :— *Brunandune* (Æthelwerd) ; *Brunanburh* (Chronicle) ; *Wendune* or *Weondune* quod alio nomine *æt Brunnanwere* (-were) vel *Brunnanbyrig* appellatur (Symeon) ; *Bruneford*, or *Brunefeld* (William of Malmesbury) ; *Brunengafeld* in the British Museum facsimile Charter ; *Brunanburgh* (R. de Hoveden) ; *Brunanburgh* approached from the Humber (Florence of Worcester) ; *Bruneswerce* (Gaimar) ; *Brunford in Northumbria* (pseudo-Ingulf) ; the plains of *Othlyn* (Ann. Clonmacnois) ; *Brune* (Ann. Camb.) ; *Dunbrunde* perhaps means this site (Pictish Chronicle) ; and *Vínheiði við Vínuskóga* is the name in Egil's Saga of the battle which corresponds in Icelandic tradition to Brunanburh in the English story. Egil's Saga also describes the battlefield as a heath between a river and a wood,

with a *borg* to the north and one on the south of the
plain ; a description which, if any confidence could be
placed in it, would help in the identification. Leland
located the scene at Brunedown, between Colyton and
Axminster, Devon ; and the Rev. C. W. Whistler
(*Saga-book of the Viking Club*, iii., p. 324) relates the
tradition of St. Catherine's chapel on Milton Hill,
Dorset, where, before the battle, Æthelstan is said to
have had his vision of victory. Old historians placed
the site at Brumby, near Doncaster : Skene found it
at Aldborough, the Roman Isurium, in Yorkshire,
equating Othlyn with Getling.   The Rev. Alfred
Hunt (British Association, 1904) contends for Burn-
ham in North Lincolnshire ; Sir J. Ramsay (*Foundations of England*, p. 285) for Bourne (Brunne) in the
south of Lincolnshire. Bromborough on the Mersey,
opposite Liverpool, has been suggested by Dr. A. C.
Gibson; but the ancient name (Mr. W. F. Irvine, *Trans.
Hist. Soc. Lanc. and Chesh.*, 1893) was Brun-bræ. Dr.
T. Hodgkin (*Hist. Eng.*, 1906) favours Burnswark.
Bromfield, Cumberland, which in the twelfth century
was Brunefeld, thus, as Rev. E. McClure points out,
preserving the name given by W. of Malmesbury, and
also the Bruningafeld of the almost contemporary
Charter, offers a possible site : but until the matter is
settled by archæological discovery we can but leave it,
with Freeman, Stubbs and Green, unsolved.

As to the persons engaged, the *Annals of Clonmacnois* have much to say. The leader of the Irish
vikings was certainly Olaf Guthfrithsson, at that time
king of Dublin, "the Red Olaf, king of Scots," of

Egil's Saga,—for Ireland was still the home of the Scots. Olaf Cuaran Sigtryggsson is not mentioned under that name, though "Awley Fivit" (Fivil? = Fífl = the Fool), numbered among the slain, may possibly stand for Olaf Cuaran, the prototype of Hamlet, and son of Sigtrygg Gale (the Crazy). It is noteworthy that one of the six Christian *landnámsmenn* of Iceland was "Ketil the Fool,"—so called, the Saga of Olaf Tryggvason says, "because he was a good Christian"; and the "folly" or "lunacy" of Sigtrygg and Olaf, who were sane enough to win kingdoms, may have been merely the heathen way of stating their conversion. Another leader was Ivar, "the King of Denmark's own son," perhaps the same with Ivar, "tanist of the Gaill," heir to the kingdom of Dublin, killed in 950. The son of Constantine, we learn, was named Ceallach. In a word, all the Vikings of Ireland and the Hebrides, together with the kingdoms of Scots and Cumbrians, attacked Æthelstan and were repulsed. It was not, however, a racial victory of Saxons or English over Scandinavians and Celts; the assistance of Viking mercenaries is hinted in Egil's Saga and corroborated by the story of Olaf Cuaran's adventure as a spy, told by William of Malmesbury, in which one of Æthelstan's staff recognised in the strange minstrel *his former captain*, but did not betray him. The Danelaw, too, was on Æthelstan's side; there is at least no indication that Northumbria and the Five Boroughs revolted before Brunanburh, or were punished afterwards; and until his death there was peace throughout the north.

Not only peace, but, according to William of Malmesbury, friendly relations with Scandinavia: " Harald, king of Norway, sent him a ship with a golden beak and a purple sail, furnished within with a compacted fence of gilded shields. The names of the persons sent with it were Helgrim and Offrid; who, being received with princely magnificence in the city of York, were amply compensated by rich presents for the labour of their journey." The story of Harald's trick, by which his youngest son Hákon was forced upon a King Æthelstan as foster-child, is referred by some to Guthorm-Æthelstan, who died 890 or 891, "or to his son and successor, who may have borne the same double name" (Green, *Conquest of England*, p. 126), and died 918. Hákon, Æthelstan's foster-son, came to the throne in Norway in 934, "and in those days was Hákon fifteen winters old" (*Heimskringla, Hákonarsaga*, i.). He was born, therefore, after the death of Guthorm II., and he lived until 960–961. On the accession of Æthelstan of England Hákon must have been five or six, according to Snorri's dating; so that the chronological difficulty is less than that which attends the invention of the name of Æthelstan for Guthorm II. of East Anglia.

On the accession of Eadmund (940) Northumbria revolted, and invited Olaf of Ireland to be king. At this time Olaf Guthfrith's son, king of Dublin, seems to have left his realm to his brother Blákári, and answered the call to York. Under him the Danes tried to regain Danish Mercia; Tamworth was stormed, but King Eadmund besieged Olaf and Wulfstan,

archbishop of York, in Leicester, until they escaped
by night from the town ; or, according to Symeon, he
intercepted them on their way to Leicester. It is
rather curious to note the attitudes of the two archbishops who arranged the peace which followed.
Wulfstan, an Englishman, was the right-hand man of
Olaf the pagan ; Odo (Oddi), a Dane by extraction
and archbishop of Canterbury, represented the Saxons.
The fusion of races had already begun, but the old
local independence survived. By the terms of the
treaty Olaf was baptised, and Ragnvald Guthfrith's
son, at a later date in the same year, was brought by
Wulfstan to Eadmund for baptism.

Olaf's baptism did not prevent him from playing
the Viking ; he raided the church of St. Balther at
Tyningham in Bernicia, and there met his death (941),
while his men ravaged and massacred at Lindisfarne.
But he was immediately succeeded by Olaf Cuaran
(Olaf with the Brogues), the son of Sigtrygg O'Ivar,
formerly of York and Dublin. He shared Northumberland with Ragnvald, who had lately been baptised,
the son of Guthfrith, and brother of the late King
Olaf. The invasion of Bernicia seems to have meant
the expulsion of the native High-reeve, or ealdorman,
Ealdred Eadulf's son, or his brother Uhtred, who had
kept up the tradition of friendship with the kings of
Wessex. It is possible that Ragnvald held this part
of Northumbria. Eadmund naturally feared the re-
construction of a great Viking power in the north,
which would give him all the work of his father and
brother to do over again ; in 944 or 945 he invaded

York, and expelled Olaf Cuaran and Ragnvald, following this action by a raid into Cumbria. There can be little doubt that his object was to break the power of the growing settlement of Vikings, of which we have seen traces in the story from the *History of St. Cuthbert*, relating to events of thirty years earlier. The story of the English chroniclers is that he fought and ousted Domhnall, son of Owain, king of Cumberland and Strathclyde, and granted the country to Malcolm, king of Scots, on condition of his alliance. In other words, he gave back to Scotland a territory which he had conquered from Scotland, but did not choose to hold as part of England ; for Cumbria was in no sense English, being inhabited by Welsh and Vikings under the tanist of the Scottish crown. To maintain any kind of English government in Cumberland and Westmorland would have been difficult and useless, but to keep down the Viking power in that region was important for the peace of England.

Olaf Cuaran's restless personality and romantic career made him the hero of legends now world-famous. Historically, so far as his biography can be summed up from Irish and English annals, he was born about 920, and after childhood at Dublin spent his boyhood at York, and early youth at the court of Constantine. In 937 he seems to have fought, but not fallen, at Brunanburh ; in 941 he became king of York. Expelled in 944 or 945, he went back to Ireland, and drove out his cousin Blákári, who had been reigning in Dublin, but does not appear to have held the kingdom long during this first tenure. In

946 we find him plundering Cill Cuilinn, and next year
attacking Dublin, where in 948 Guthfrith Sigtryggson
was reigning, that is to say, Olaf Cuaran's brother.
In 949 Olaf returned to York, where he reigned until
952. Next year he was plundering near Donard, in
co. Wicklow, and sacking Inisdowill. In 956 Olaf
Guthfrithsson the younger, lord of the Gaill at Dublin,
won a great battle over the Irish; perhaps this was a
nephew of Olaf Cuaran acting as his general. In 961
Olaf, King of Dublin (Cuaran?) was attacked by
Sigtrygg Cam, a Viking from overseas, and being
wounded in the thigh with an arrow, escaped with
loss. In 964 Olaf (Cuaran) Sigtryggsson was defeated
in Kilkenny, but in 970 he plundered Kells, and in
977 slew the two heirs (tanists) of Ireland, Muirchear-
tach and Conghalach. The great battle of Tara, 979,
in which King Maelseachlann defeated him and
killed his son Ragnvald, broke his power; next year
he retired to Iona, where he died in 981. By his
second wife, Gormflaith, he had a son, Sigtrygg Silki-
skeggi (Silk-beard), who became king of Dublin;
other sons were Gluniarainn (Járn-kné) and Harald.
Duald mac Firbis says that in his time, the seventeenth
century, most of the Dublin merchants traced their
pedigree to Olaf Cuaran. His name, Amhlaeibh in
Irish, became Abloic in Welsh (the language of
Strathclyde), whence the legends of Havelock Cuhe-
ran the Dane, and according to Professor I. Gollancz
(*Hamlet in Iceland*, Introduction), the traditions about
him and his family became the groundwork of the
tale of Hamlet, prince of Denmark.

When Eadred came to the English throne in 946
archbishop Wulfstan and two Northumbrian jarls,
"Imorcer and Andcoll," joined in his election ; but it
does not seem to have satisfied the Northumbrian
people, for a year or two later he marched to Tad-
denesscylfe (Tanshelf, Pontefract ?), where Wulfstan
and the Northumbrian Witan swore fidelity to him.
In the same year, however, they elected one Eirík as
king.   The identity of this Eirík, and the sequence
of events, cannot be easily discussed in a paragraph ;
but elsewhere (*Saga-book of the Viking Club*, ii., pp.
313–327, and *Trans. Cumb. and West. Antiq. Soc.*, N.S.,
ii., pp. 231–241) reasons are given for accepting the
account of Snorri Sturluson and the Norse historians,
who make him the famous Eirík Blódöx, son of
Harald Fairhair of Norway, as against that of Adam
of Bremen, who makes this king of Northumbria to
be Hiring, son of Harald Blátönn, king of Denmark.
Mr. J. R. Green (*Conquest of England*, pp. 262 *seq.*,
289 *seq.*) tried to combine both stories, making
Harald Blátönn attempt to place his son on the
throne of York in 947, (though there is no sign that
his fleet, even if it was off Normandy in 945, ever
touched English shores,) and finding a place for
Eirík Blódöx, son of Harald Fairhair, in the years
after Brunanburh (though there is no mention of
any such king in Northumbria at that time in any
British chronicle).   The events as given in the English annals are :—947, the Northumbrians belied the
oath which they had just sworn to King Eadred, im-
plying that they set up the king mentioned in 948

as Yric ; Eadred ravaged their country and burned St. Wilfrith's minster at Ripon, then marched away, but his rearguard being cut up at Chesterford, he returned, and was received as king, "Hyryc" being expelled ; in 949 Anlaf Cwiran (Olaf Cuaran) came to Northumberland ; in 952 Yric supplanted him as king, and was expelled in 954.

Later authors do not improve matters by trying to simplify the story, which ended with the death of Eirík in an attempt to regain his throne, and the appointment of Oswulf of Bamborough, a representative of the old line of Bernician Angles, as jarl or ealdorman of Northumbria. Olaf Cuaran went back to Dublin, where, on his expulsion from York in 945, he had seized the power after driving out Blákári. It was perhaps before this that St. Cathroë (see his life in *The Chronicles of the Picts and Scots*, ed. Skene, p. 116) was escorted by King Domhnall of Cumbria to Leeds, and thence went to York to visit the king, whose name is given as Erichius, and his Irish wife, a relative of the saint. As Eirík had no Irish wife, but Olaf Cuaran and his predecessor Olaf were married to Irish ladies, King Olaf and not Eirík is no doubt intended. The story of Egil Skallagrímsson's visit to King Eirík Blódöx at York is not impossible, though romantic in character, and though the poem attributed to the skald on this occasion, *Höfudlausn*, contains the end-rhymes which are thought to mark verse of a later date. These incidents give colour to the meagre records of the Viking court, at which so many races and interests must have met.

In the grave-monuments showing wheel-crosses and
other motives derived from Irish and Scottish art,
and in the curious carved bone from York, figured
in *The Reliquary* for Oct. 1904, we see evidence
of the connexion between Northumbria and the
Celtic lands ; the Reycross at Stainmoor, as far as its
original form can be determined from its damaged
remains and from seventeenth-century descriptions,
must have been of the type in vogue about the middle
of the tenth century, and may be conjectured—though
such conjectures are not legitimate archæology—to be
a memorial of the great battle of Stainmoor (954 ?),
which ended the life of Eirík Blódöx and the independence of the Viking kingdom of Northumbria.
A finer and more authentic memorial is the " Eiríks-
mál ; " see *Corpus Poeticum Boreale* (i., p. 260) and
the paraphrase in Dasent's *Burnt Njál* (ii., p. 384)
which describes Odin awaking in Valhöll, and bidding
his heroes make ready to welcome Eirík and the five
kings who fell with him.

The spirit of local independence was not dead,
for on the accession of the boy-king Eadwig, in
957, Mercia and Northumbria revolted, and invited
his brother Eadgar, a still younger boy, but one
with more tact and spirit, to be their king. The
revolution was effected without war. For two
years Eadgar was independent ruler of Danish England, while Bernicia still remained Anglian under
Oswulf. Under Eadgar's rule influences from the
south of England doubtless improved the growing
civilisation and prosperity of Yorkshire. No great

abbeys were yet founded in the north ; but the work
of rebuilding churches, which had begun in the
southern part of the Danelaw, must have made progress. It was not until 970 that Ely was restored as
a monastery. The Danes were at first destroyers,
though Wilfrith's Ripon survived their attacks until
Eadred destroyed it ; they were no architects or
masons, and their earlier monuments in imitation of
the beautiful Anglian crosses were mere slabs picked
from the surface of rocky land and chipped over with
a pattern ; their churches were thatched or tiled
fabrics of wood or wattle-and-daub, such as the hogback tombs represent. But after the middle of the
century their monuments seem to have become more
skilfully quarried and carved, though still with the
Anglo-Danish style of ornament, unlike the art of
southern England at the time ; and it is possible that
some of the "Saxon" churches of the north were
restored, and others built, under the influence of the
revival of arts in the reign of Eadgar.

When he succeeded his brother on the throne of all
England (959) the Danelaw, in a sense, gave a king
to the Saxons, and with him Anglo-Danes won places
in church and state. We have seen that Odo could
rise to an archbishopric ; now his nephew Oswald
became bishop of Worcester, and, after Oskytel
(Ásketil), archbishop of York. Thord Gunnarsson,
who led the English expedition into Cumbrian and
Viking Westmorland in 966, and was afterwards jarl
of Deira, was already, in 961, "præpositus domus" of
the king ; and many Scandinavian names appear in

the lists of witnesses to royal charters. Eadgar's laws
left the Northumbrian Danes in possession of their
old rights and usages, and his policy encouraged
intercourse with foreigners; so much indeed that
both the old poem quoted in the Chronicle and the
account of his reign by William of Malmesbury make
against him the charge, so often repeated in English
history, that " outlandish men he hither enticed,
and harmful people allured to this land." It was
said that when Eadred held his court at Abingdon
the Northumbrian visitors became so drunk by
nightfall that they had to retire ; and that, under
Eadgar, the Saxons—" though they were free from
such propensities before that time "—learned drunken-
ness from the Danes. On the other hand, John
of Wallingford's story of the reason why the Danes
were hated is not without significance :—" they were
wont, after the fashion of their country, to comb
their hair every day, to bathe every Saturday "—
Laugardag, " bath-day,"—" to change their garments
often, and set off their persons by many such frivolous
devices. In this manner they laid siege to the virtue
of the women." Freeman always represents the
Northumbrian Danes as barbarians, but it does not
appear that the charge is justified.

5. SVEIN AND KNÚT.

The story of Scandinavian England in the eleventh
century divides itself naturally into two parts—the
invasion of Svein and Knút ; and the fruitless attempt

of Harald Hardrádi, followed by the tragic last scene in which William the Norman put an end to the power of the old Viking colony.

Southern England had been free from war and piracy for eighty years. Æthelred the "Ill-advised" had recently been crowned, a boy of ten or eleven; Dunstan had retired from the government, but the old times of viking raids appeared to be past, and the horizon was as unclouded as ever it is on the day before a storm. In 980 a small party of Danes attacked Southampton, and then Thanet; Cheshire also was raided. In 981 the same Danes ravaged Devon and Cornwall. In 982 they harried Portland. The leader in these new attacks must have been Svein Tjúguskeggi ("with the forked beard"), son of Harald Blátönn, king of Denmark. He had been forcibly baptised when Otto the Great invaded Denmark, but in earlier years made no pretence of Christianity nor of filial devotion, and went viking with his friend Pálnatóki (of Wales, and later of Jómsborg) until the death of Harald in 986.

In 985 the Mercian ealdorman Ælfric, being banished, fled to Denmark. To Normandy English refugees had already betaken themselves, and in 991 Duke Richard I. and Æthelred made a treaty by which they agreed not to harbour fugitives across the Channel; but this proved of no more effect than to show that the respective governments had some idea of common action in the matter of outlaws turned vikings. That an English nobleman should take refuge in Denmark shows new relations between

K

England and the Scandinavian lands, soon to be
brought into closer connexion.

Another country came into view, so to speak, from
the shores of southern England when vikings from
Norway began to be recognised among the invaders.
On the west coast the Norse were well known ; Ælfred
had written of his visitors from Halogaland and the
Baltic ; traders from the fjords had taken cargoes to
English ports, and among the hosts of earlier years
many a Norseman had been numbered. But so far
no distinctly Norwegian army had attacked southern
England. In 991 Jóstein (Justin) and Guthmund
plundered Ipswich ; they are called Danes, and Justin
is a Danish form of the name ; but a Jóstein was
maternal uncle of King Olaf Tryggvason, who joined
this party, and Guthmund is called Justin's brother.

At Maldon they overthrew the Essex levies under
Brihtnoth, in a battle made famous by the ballad
which tells how the bridge was defended by three
champions, one of whom—from his name Maccus—
seems to have been of Viking origin himself. One
result of this battle was the first payment of
that enormous Danegeld which soon became the
chief feature of these new invasions. On this
occasion archbishop Sigeric, ealdorman Æthelwerd
the chronicler, and Ælfric of Hampshire were the
negotiators on the English side ; they have borne the
blame of initiating the weak and disastrous course of
money-payments which tempted Viking attacks. But
it was no new thing. From 865 onwards such black-
mail was levied. Freeman notes a bequest to Hyde

of money "to keep hunger, and heathen men if need
be, from the Abbey." Meredith of Wales (989) paid
a penny a head for his subjects to ransom them from
the Black Army. The new Danegeld was the old
payment on a larger scale and in a more business-like
style. The sums exacted were increased to an extent
which seems almost fabulous, considering the rateable
value of land, and they could only have been raised
by recourse to the treasures of monasteries, churches
and the wealthy, in days when hoards of gold and
silver made up into valuable shrines, book-covers,
furniture and personal ornaments were the chief and
most available form of riches. The work of the
Saxon gold- and silver-smiths, to judge from its
remains, was highly artistic and intrinsically valuable.
It must have been weighed out by the pound,
perhaps melted down or broken up, for the Vikings;
for all the hoards of English coins found in Scandinavia, with all that may be imagined as lost and still
to seek, or spent and again circulated, would be
only as a drop in the bucket to the sums they are
said to have received. After £10,000 in 991,
£16,000 was paid in 994, £24,000 in 1002, £30,000
in 1007, and in 1009 East Kent paid £3,000. In
1014 the sum of £21,000 was paid; in 1018 Knút,
when newly crowned, took £72,000, beside £11,000
paid by the Londoners alone. In 1040 Hördaknút
took £21,099, beside £11,048 paid for thirty-two
ships. With a Dane upon the throne the Danegeld
seems to have become an occasional war-tax, but it
was levied more than once by the Confessor, who is

said to have abolished it about 1051, but William the
Conqueror levied a similar tax when he was crowned,
and another in the following year, and again another
in 1083–1084. Prof. Maitland (*Domesday Book and
Beyond*, p. 6) calls the sums exacted under Æthelred
and Knút "appalling." At two shillings the hide,
which was worth about a pound, England in the
middle of the twelfth century could pay only £5198 ;
so that £30,000 would be half the total value of the
kingdom, unless it was richer in the tenth than in
the twelfth century, or unless recourse could be had
to the hoarded wealth of many ancestral treasuries.
It must be remembered, however, that some of the
Viking hosts remained for a considerable time in the
country ; buccaneers are often open-handed, and much
of their prize-money must have gone back to the
people of the towns where they took up their
quarters.

After the battle of Maldon, Olaf Tryggvason himself joined his kinsmen, and the host was enlisted by
the Saxon Witan to remain and defend Wessex from
the Danes. A further sum of £22,000 is said to have
been paid as a retaining fee, beside salaries while
they were on active service : but at the same time
they were allowed in certain cases to wage war or
make raids on other parts of the island, and any
province making a separate treaty with them was to
be outlawed. So next year we find a great fleet in
the English service on the Thames, commanded by
Thord of York, Ælfric, formerly a refugee in Denmark,
and two bishops. It is not surprising that Ælfric first

warned and then joined the Danes, and that their
attack though fruitless was not wholly disastrous to
them. We hear no more of this Ælfric, whose ship
was captured ; and we hear no more of jarl Thord of
York, whose place was shortly afterwards filled by
Waltheof I. as ruler of Bernicia, and by Ælfhelm in
Deira.

In 993 the coast from Bamborough to Lindsey was
ravaged : the "English" leaders, two of whom bore
Danish names, deserted their levies, and the Vikings
had a free course. Next year Olaf Tryggvason,
no longer the mercenary of Wessex, joined forces
with Svein, king of Denmark, to conquer England.
On September 8, 994, they attacked London, but
were repulsed ; they ravaged the shores of the
Thames, and Canterbury was saved only by the payment of 90 pounds of silver and 400 ounces of gold.
Then they plundered Essex, Kent, Sussex, and Hampshire, and were bought off at Southampton by a payment of £16,000 levied on all England, and a regular
stipend to be paid by Wessex alone. After the conclusion of the treaty Olaf Tryggvason was brought by
bishop Ælfheah and our chronicler Æthelwerd to
Andover, where he was confirmed in the presence of
King Æthelred. According to his saga he had been
baptised by a hermit on the "Syllingar," perhaps the
Scilly Islands, or possibly (as a famous abbot and
a great cloister are mentioned) one of the island
monasteries of Ireland ; the geography of the sagas,
when it relates to Britain, is often defective, while the
incidents may contain a true tradition. At Andover,

as the Chronicle records to his honour, " he made a
covenant with King Æthelred, even as he also fulfilled,
that he never again would come as an enemy to the
English nation."

Svein went to the Isle of Man, but the bulk of the
army, who had remained at Southampton and were
supposed to be in the English service, ravaged Cornwall and Devon, burnt Tavistock Abbey, and then
harried Dorset and the Isle of Wight. Next year
they sailed up the Medway, besieged Rochester and
plundered in Kent. In this they were probably within
the meaning of the act, as they understood it : the
west, and Kent, were not the country they had undertaken to guard ; and it is to be borne in mind that
we have the story from one side only. There was
evasion of payment on several occasions in the account
of Saxon dealings with the Vikings ; and the local
jealousies of England suggest that one district was
sometimes not entirely displeased to see another
victimised.

It has been suggested (Sir J. Ramsay, *Foundations
of England*, p. 340) that the Scandinavian settlements
in the Lake district date from this time : Thietmar of
Merseburg speaks of territory assigned to invading
bands for permanent occupation, and Jóstein and
Guthmund henceforward disappear from history " as
if they had found comfortable quarters somewhere."
But the Lake district was not in Æthelred's realm ;
the quarters assigned seem to have been in and
near Southampton. Æthelred ravaged Cumberland
a few years later, as he would hardly have done if

settlers in his pay and on lands granted by him had occupied it. The wild dales would not have afforded comfortable quarters to men who had come for plunder, and no place-names record Jóstein and Guthmund, as might be expected, if two chiefs so noted had settled there; a "Godmond Hall" near Kendal is of much later origin. We shall see reasons for dating the Cumbrian settlement much earlier, and Olaf's uncle Jóstein, according to the saga, accompanied him home and stood by him to the end.

In the year 1000 the troublesome host sailed to Normandy. Æthelred took advantage of their absence for his expedition to Cumberland, where already there must have been a colony which threatened the peace of the north. Some Vikings, however, were still in the English service, chief of whom was Pallig, the husband of King Svein's sister Gunnhild. Æthelred appears to have entertained some idea of forming a permanent army, more efficient than the temporary levies; but the error lay in over-estimating the trust-worthiness of mercenaries who were tempted by opportunities for plunder in the wealthy, easy-going districts around them, and, as the sequel shows, were treated with a want of confidence ending in the atrocious massacre of St. Brice. Pallig's men were ill kept in hand; there was plundering and fighting; the Saxons believed that they intended to kill the king and the Witan and to seize the kingdom. The Witan met and commissioned Leofsige, ealdorman of Essex, to treat with the turbulent strangers. They asked a subsidy of £24,000; but Leofsige himself, in the act of negotiation, committed a murder for which he was outlawed. Then it was resolved to meet plot with plot, and kill off all the Danes in England, or at least all those of Pallig's command. The massacre of St. Brice's day (November 12, 1002) has been reduced to its lowest terms by Freeman, but that it struck the English themselves with horror and shame is evident. Henry of Huntingdon records that in his boyhood, eighty years later, the event was still remembered in common talk. At Oxford the sanctuary of the church was as little respected by the English as ever it had been by the Vikings : St. Frideswide's was burnt with all the Danes who had taken refuge in it. It was the common reproach that the Vikings spared neither age nor sex : but now the English beheaded Gunnhild, a royal princess, a Christian, and a hostage, after both her husband, jarl Pallig, and her son had been killed before her eyes. If the circumstances of this, which all England might have regarded as a natural and laudable act of vengeance, have been exaggerated, what are we to think of the chroniclers' stories of Viking crime but that they must be taken with great abatement?

The massacre was "not only a crime but a blunder," as Freeman remarks, and it brought a speedy revenge. Next year Svein, now king of Denmark and Norway, invaded and took Exeter, Wilton, and Old Sarum ; in 1004 he sacked Norwich, and overcame the East Anglian fyrd under Ulfketil, the old ealdorman's right-hand man, the Ulfkell Snillingr of the sagas, a true English patriot though his name betrays a Viking

origin. In 1005 a famine sent the Danes away, only
to return in 1006 when they ravaged Kent and Sussex,
wintered in the Isle of Wight, and next year marched
to Reading and Marlborough; but on payment of
£36,000 they desisted from further attacks for the
time. In 1008 a great fleet was got together by the
English, but Wulfnoth of Sussex, being impeached
before the king, turned viking, and defied the whole
power of the country.

Two fleets arrived at Sandwich in 1009, one
under Hemming and Eylaf and the other under
Thorkel the Tall, son of Strut-Harald, jarl of Sjæland,
and brother of Hemming. Taking a ransom of
£3,000 for Canterbury, they plundered the south
coast, and wintered in their burg at Greenwich. Next
year they made four raids into the interior, in the first
of which Ulfketil offered an unsuccessful resistance
at Ringmere (near Thetford?): but as the year pro-
ceeded the defence became weaker, until at last the
Witan negotiated for peace at the price of £48,000.
The payment was delayed: meantime Canterbury
was attacked—it is evident that Canterbury was not
in the area affected by the negotiations—and the
whole population was held to ransom. It was not
until the Easter of next year that the first debt was
paid, and the payment celebrated at a feast in which
the Viking soldiers—Thorkel himself, it is said, being
absent—drank themselves drunk on wine, and dragged
archbishop Ælfheah to their " husting " clamouring
for the ransom of Canterbury. On his refusal they
pelted him with bones from their feast, and one of them

named Thrym ("stupid"), who had been lately confirmed by Ælfheah himself, put him out of his misery
with the stroke of an axe. Thorkel did what he could
to make amends for the "regrettable incident," in
which the Danes too completely justified the charges
laid against them. He gave up the body of the archbishop for honourable burial, and shortly took service
under the English king, whom he supported with
fidelity until the flight to Normandy, which put an
end to Æthelred's actual reign.

During 1013 King Svein arrived once more with a
great fleet. With him, or about this time, arrived
Olaf Haraldsson, afterwards king and saint, but
certainly during all this period engaged in viking
exploits. Some years later, when Olaf was king of
Norway, the skald Ottar the Black made a love-song
to the queen, for which he was condemned to
death; he won his life by composing a poem on the
king's deeds in England, mentioning especially the
breaking of London Bridge, the battle of Ringmere,
and the capture of Canterbury. According to Snorri
Sturluson he fought for the English against the
Danes, but the circumstances are not easy to make
out.

Uhtred, the Anglo-Danish governor of Northumbria,
set the example of adherence to Svein, and all the
north of England followed. Marching through Mercia,
the Danes met no resistance until they were repulsed
from London by the townsfolk under Thorkel, but
even London opened its gates to them when the
Witan had met in the west, and by its submission

Svein had become *de facto* king of England. Thorkel's fleet of Danish mercenaries was the only refuge for Æthelred, who followed his queen and family to Normandy in January 1014. On February 3 King Svein died.

Knút, son of Svein, succeeded him in the kingdom of England, not without severe opposition on the part of the English, which forced him at first to take ship for Denmark. Finding Harald, his brother, already on the Danish throne, he returned in 1015 to England to recover his father's realm. Olaf Haraldsson for some little time remained in England; whatever side he may have taken previously, it was he who brought back Æthelred from Normandy on the death of Svein. But Æthelred was already dying. His son, Eadmund Ironside, estranged from him, and finding assistance from none but his brother-in-law, Uhtred of Northumbria, kept up some show of resistance until Knút marched to York and Uhtred gave up the contest. On April 23, 1016, Æthelred died, and all England, except London, adhered to the Dane. Knút brought his fleet to Greenwich, and besieged Eadmund in the city, cutting a canal through the marshes of Southwark in order to tow his ships above London Bridge, and then making a dyke round the north side of the walls to complete the blockade. Eadmund escaped, and gathered troops in the west, fought a notable series of battles at Penselwood, Sherstone, London, and Brentwood, driving the Danes down to the coast of Kent, and defeating them in a battle at Otford. They withdrew into Sheppey and thence into Essex,

where Eadmund met them once more at Assandun,
and lost the last decisive action. The site of Assandan
is usually placed at Ashingdon, because Canewdon—
quasi Canute-don—is near it; but the names in
Domesday are *Ascenduna*, which does not tally with
Assandun, and *Carendun*. Ashdon, near Saffron
Walden, has been suggested, but the circumstances
of the battle appear to fit Sandon, near Danbury,
"the Danes' burg," on the road between Maldon and
Chelmsford, along which Knút's men were probably
returning from their raid into "Mercia," which may
mean Mersea in Essex.

After this great overthrow it was useless for Eadmund
Ironside to resist. Knút proposed a meeting at
"Olanege," near "Deorhyrst," on the Severn, where
the two kings "became fellows and pledge-brothers."
They agreed to divide England, Eadmund taking
Wessex and paying a Danegeld. But on November
30, 1016, he died—murdered, his partisans held, at
the instigation of Knút—and the Vikings at last ruled
the country they had sought for two centuries to
conquer.

In the "Lithsmen's Song," made by the men of the
host, *Skjöldunga saga* says, though the saga of St.
Olaf attributes it to the king and saint himself, we
have a curious and valuable echo of the time. We
see how the Vikings looked upon their adventure; we
get the touch of nature which brings the "fury of the
Northman" before us in a new light, and reveals no
hero, no demon, but just the Tommy Atkins of a
barrack-room ballad, with his two themes of song—

the glory of the service and the girl he left behind
him. For the text, see *Corpus Poeticum Boreale*, ii.,
pp. 106–108 ; but the bald abstract there given hardly
renders the spirit of the original :—

Marching up the country,—on ! before they know
Deeds are doing, shields are shining, roofs are lying low ;
Up, heart ! wave and waft the weapon of Odin's Maid,
And the English throng will hurry along in flight before the
blade.

There's many a man in the realm where we were bred and
born
Has donned his easy old coat and flytes his fellow this very
morn ;
While here's a lad in a shirt of steel the smith with his hammer
has sewed
Goes singing abroad to feed the crows their fill of English
blood.

There's one in the glad of the gloaming—what cares he forth
to roam ?
He's shy to redden the scathe of shields—he kisses a girl at
home ;
He'll carry no shield to England for glory and gold this year,
But bides with Steinvör, North of Stad,—in Norway with my
dear.

'Thought me, when I spied them, Thorkel's folk were fain
—The song of the sword they never shirk—to tread the battle-
plain ;
And awhile ago at Ringmere Heath we pushed into the fray,
We stood the storm of iron, with our host in war-array.

So the song goes on, with reminiscences of Ulfketil,
who gave them a good fight, but "changed his mind"
and fled ; of Knút, the trusty leader, sharing the
soldiers' danger—

Knút gave the word,—he bade us make a stand ;
He held a shield among us when we fought by London
strand ;

—the battle at the dyke, the scene of the ships passing

the canal, and the assaults on the city walls. Then it
reverts to the girl at home—poor thing !—mated to
the laggard and pining away like the leaves of the
linden in autumn ; and concludes—

> Day by day the buckler was reddened with reeking gore,
> When we were out on the foray with our champion in the
> war :
> But now that the war is over and the last hard fight is won,
> Merry we sit as the days go by in fair London-town.

So also the treachery and cruelty laid to Knút's
charge, especially in his earlier years, disappear almost
to vanishing point on examination. Nor, on the other
hand, was he a great beneficent power, always listen-
ing to the merry song of monks and rebuking his
courtiers for their flattery. He was very shrewd ; all the
chess-playing cleverness of the Viking intellect was
shown in his strategy and administration. It mattered
not whether his chessmen were Danish or English
—"Northman" of the Hwiccas, even jarl Eirík, jarl
Hákon Eiríksson and Thorkel were sacrificed, Eadulf
Cudel the Angle and Godwine the Saxon were advanced, when the game required. Not to press a
powerful family to revolt, he would favour one member
of it when he had removed another : in 1020 Æthelwerd the ealdorman was banished, and his brother-in-
law Æthelnoth was promoted to the archbishopric.
For the sake of policy Knút in his youth appears to
have married Ælfgifu of Northampton, daughter of
Ælfhelm, ealdorman of Deira ; but in 1017 he married
Emma of Normandy, Æthelred's widow. In matters
of religion he showed himself almost ostentatiously

zealous; especially honouring St. Cuthbert, St. Eadmund, the martyr of the early Vikings, St. Ælfheah,
the victim of his own comrades; and in 1026 going
on pilgrimage to Rome, not without an eye to diplo-
matic business, for the journey enabled him to attend
the coronation of the Emperor Conrad, with whom he
arranged the marriage of his daughter Gunnhild to
the heir of Germany; and he was able also to get
various concessions from the pope and the king of
Burgundy, advantageous to English and Danes on
pilgrimage or on business abroad. As a legislator and
military organiser he found the happy mean between
Danish and English interests. He did not rule in any
altruistic spirit, for he exacted enormous sums of
money from the conquered nation; nor did he throw
himself on the country which he adopted as his own
without the new safeguard of an efficient standing
army; but he gave justice, peace and well-being such
as England had not known for a generation.

Knút's Laws, which Freeman thought to date from
the end of his reign (after 1028), because they mention
Peter's Pence and Knút's title of King of Norway,
begin with admonitions to religious duty—to fear God,
hold one Christian belief, and love King Knút with
true faith; to keep the feasts of Eadward, king and
martyr, and of Dunstan the bishop; to observe
Sunday; to forsake idols and the worship of sun and
moon, fire and water, wells, stones and trees. The
second part, dealing with secular matters, re-enacts
with some additions the laws of former kings of
England: Eadgar's recognition of the local rights of

the Danelaw, Mercia and Wessex was repeated.   The
general lines of government and society already laid
down are followed without much change, though there
is a tendency to closer organisation—not a new thing,
but leading in the direction of feudalism.   It used to
be thought, for example, that private jurisdiction came
in with Knút, but Professor Maitland (*Domesday Book
and Beyond*, p. 282) has shown that express grants of
sac and soc were known in the tenth century.   Under
Knút, however, the mutual responsibility on which
order and justice were based seems to have become
rather more territorial than merely personal ; every
freeman over twelve years of age was to be enrolled in
a Hundred and Tithing.[1]   The hundred court had
to see justice done, failing which the king's justice
could be appealed to ; he alone could decide cases
involving outlawry, and had the dues in certain causes,
such as highway robbery (whence "the king's highway"), and other breaches of the peace not covered
by the popular courts.   In the county court the bishop
and the ealdorman still presided, no distinction being
made between the administration of ecclesiastical and
that of secular law.   Nor was any distinction made to

---

[1] Bishop Stubbs (*Const. Hist.*, i. p. 94) says that in the so-
called Laws of Edward the Confessor, a twelfth-century compila-
tion based on the Laws of Knút, men were bound to associate
in groups of ten, called *frithborh* in the south, but *tenmannetale*
in the north ; adding that *tenmentale* in Richmondshire was,
temp. Henry II., an extent of fourteen carucates, paying 4s. 7d.
annual tax.   Maitland (*Domesday Book*, p. 387) remarks that
the unit of land in Sweden is the *mantal*.   We may add that
manntal in the old Icelandic law means a "muster, census,"
which may explain *tenmantal=frithborh*, *temp.* Knút.

give Knút's victorious army a preference over the conquered country; they had not even "sporting rights,"
in spite of a severe hunting-code which is attributed
in error to this period; every man could hunt on his
own ground, except where the king had made a royal
forest. The slave-trade was forbidden, and if the
punishment of adulteresses by the loss of nose and
ears seems severe, on the other hand Knút did not
claim the right of selling the hand of a woman in
marriage, as was the custom later, and it was provided
that no wife should be held an accomplice of her
husband in a case of theft unless the goods were
found in her store-room, locked cupboard, or private
bag. It is not wonderful if, as Freeman says, "after
Knút's power was once fully established, we hear no
complaint against his government from any trustworthy
English source."

Knút's standing army was an improvement upon
the tentative measures in that direction framed by
Ælfred, and a great advance upon the merely mercenary troops of aliens from time to time engaged by
Æthelred and his predecessors. It was a development of the Vikings' permanent crews of enlisted
men, picked and trained and paid for their work.
They were known as the king's *húskarls*, a word
which, like Northman, Lochlann, Sumarlidi, Viking,
etc., became a personal name. The nucleus of this
force was formed in 1018 by the crews of forty ships,
but it is not easy to reckon the number of men to
which these crews would amount. Knút's marine
army was reckoned by "rowlocks"; the pay was

L

eight marks Anglo-Saxon (= £4) " æt ælcere hame-
lan," a word which has puzzled English historians, but
represents the Icelandic *hamla*, the oar-loop which holds
the oar to the thole (*hár*) in the Viking ship.   In
Norway, a levy was counted, not by men, but by *hömlur*,
and the number of men was of course greater, for there
must have been relays of rowers on a long voyage, or
at least a considerable percentage of substitutes.   In
fact the reckoning represented the size of the vessel,
its tonnage, so to say : and as Florence of Worcester
mentions a ship given by Godwine to Hördaknút with
80 rowers, the ships of Thorkel and Knút may have
been much larger than the Gokstad boat of the quite
early Viking time.   This would raise the number of
Knút's *hirð* to over 3000 " rowlocks."

From a Danish code of the twelfth century, as well as
from such descriptions as that of the Jómsviking settlement, we gather that these professional soldiers had
a stringent set of customs of their own.   The relations
of lord and man were strictly defined ; the dealings of
members of the crew with one another, and their
detachment from the world of civilians, were set forth.
That sucn laws, which in the *Viðrlags-rétt* (code of
penalties) are ascribed somewhat doubtfully to this
King Knút, did actually hold good in his days appears
to be proved from the story which tells how he once,
in a fit of anger, killed one of his men, and condemned
himself in the húskarls' court to pay the accustomed
penalty nine times over.   That such a standing force
should not be popular, and that there were tales of
their arrogance and oppression, is natural ; but when

Knút sent away the greater part of his army, and retained only these húskarls, the Witan promised that they should " have firm peace "; that any Englishman who killed one of them should be punished, and if he was not found his Hundred or township should pay the blood-money.

Knút died Nov. 12, 1035, master, as his father was, but far more effectively master of England, Denmark and Norway. He cannot have intended to form a permanent empire; in those days personal allegiance of the local rulers was everything; imperial organisation was hardly within practical politics. Bernicia, much diminished by the loss of the Lothians, was still in the hands of the old Anglian family which had survived all the Viking invasions, and was now represented by Ealdred, Uhtred's son, and at his death by his brother Eadwulf. Deira was ruled in 1033 by Siward the Stout (Sigurd Digri) an Anglo-Dane who had married Æthelflæd, daughter of jarl Ealdred. Mercia was still under Leofric, and Wessex under Godwine; Hereford and Eastern Mercia were under Ranig and Thurig or Thórir. The kingdom of England had been promised by Knút to Emma's son Hördaknút, but he was now ruling Denmark; Svein, the eldest son of Knút's first marriage, was in Norway; and his brother Harald Harefoot, being on the spot, and half a Northumbrian, was elected by the vote of the Northumbrians and Londoners (or the standing army in London, the *liðsmenn*, not necessarily the " nautic multitude " as Freeman took it). Godwine and Wessex stood for Hördaknút, and it was not until the attempt of the ætheling Ælfred and the atrocity which put an end to it—an atrocity, the chroniclers say, worse than any charged to the Vikings —that Harald was accepted as king over all England. In this respect the story of Eadgar was repeated ; the Danish north again gave a king to the south.

Harald Harefoot spent his time—Sundays included —in hunting : he reduced the húskarl army, picked no quarrels, and the land had rest, but for a little border fighting, until he died in 1040. Hördaknút, Emma's son and king of Denmark was then elected, King Stork after King Log. He began by disinterring the body of his brother Harald and throwing it into the town ditch ; the Londoners rescued the body and buried it in St. Clement Danes, then a suburban church, built, as its name implies, for the Scandinavian population. That there were Danes buried within the city also is shown by the monument now in the Guildhall Museum and found in St. Paul's churchyard, a sculptured stone of the eleventh century, not without some traces of Irish influence in its style, with runes " [To the memory of some man unknown] his wife let this stone be raised ; also Tuki." The subject of the panel is the well-known emblem of the Hart and Hound, symbolising, it is thought, the Christian in persecution ; a strange epitaph, one would think, for one of the " proud invaders," and yet very frequently used. It is perhaps possible that the ancient emblem of the Danish capital at Leira, the hart, lingered in tradition, and fixed this particular form as a popular

one in monumental masonry : it is possible also that
epitaphs then—expressed in pictorial form and not
until rather later in the set phrase of eulogy seen on
Manx and Scandinavian stones—were as little related
to biographical fact as those of any country churchyard.
And yet the sentiment conveyed by the Viking Age
tombstones, like that of the Christian Skaldic songs, is
strikingly akin to the piety of all ages.   The struggle
with the Serpent, hardly vanquished ; the Cross
triumphant over powers of sin and death ; symbols
of resignation and resurrection,—on these mainly
the design depends in all its various forms ; rarely
showing something that may be intended for a portrait
effigy, still less commonly anything like the heraldic
ostentation of a later age or the hint of a warrior's
fame.   It is interesting to infer the character of the
people who put up these monuments—the more tender
and sincere side of the deep Scandinavian nature.

The great preponderance of Scandinavian blood in
the north of England is shown by the list of
"festermen," or those who gave pledges (borh) for
Archbishop Ælfric at his election to the see of York
in 1023.   The list is contemporary, written on the fly-
leaf of a tenth-century MS. Gospels in the library of
York Minster.   It has been published by Prof.
G. Stephens, and more recently with analysis of
the names by Dr. Jón Stefánsson (*Saga-book of the
Viking Club*, 1906), who remarks that the place-names
seem to be from South Yorkshire, and that many of the
personal names are more Norse than Danish.   The
termination -ketil, used in the earlier part of the

eleventh century by Norwegians and Icelanders, had been shortened by that time to -kil or -kel in Danish and Swedish, and the full form is found here in Alfcetel, Arcetel, Ascetel, Audcetel, Cetel, Grimcetel, Roscetel, Ulfcetel, Thorcetel. Judged by their occurrence elsewhere some of the names represent Norwegians rather than Danes :—Asbeorn, Beorn, Barad, Blih (Blígr), Colbrand, Berhdor (Bergthor), Halwærd (Hallvard), Raganald, Tholf (Thórólf); others are rather Danish than Norse :—Fardain (equivalent to Farman, " trader "), Folcer, Merlesuuan, Siuerd, Snel ; while the rest of those which are not Anglo-Saxon may be either Danish or Norse :—Ailaf, Ana, Arner (Arnthor), Asmund, Forna, Gamal, Grim, Gunner, Háwer (Hávard), Justan, Lefer (Leifr), Osulf, Ulf, Ulfer, Thor (Thórir). Many more Old Norse names are given in the Durham *Liber Vitæ*, the earliest part of which is of the tenth century. Dr. Stefánsson thinks that the Norse element here represented had been long in Yorkshire, and not recently come in with jarl Eirík Hákonarson. In that case, however, one would expect their language and names to have been assimilated to the general use in Northumbria at the time, and not to show dialectic differences lately evolved in the homes they had left many generations earlier. Travel and trade must have already brought Norwegians into England, but we must be careful not to over-estimate the Norse in Yorkshire at this date, remembering that forty years later Norwegians were received as enemies but Danes as friends.

Hördaknút was as unfavourable an example of a

Viking ruler as his father had been the reverse.
Soured by ill-health and the spoilt child of an ambitious
and often disappointed mother, king of Denmark in
his " teens " and king of England also at twenty or
twenty-one, he spent his short reign in exactions,
quarrels and violent revenges, and died suddenly, as
every schoolboy reads, after drinking at a wedding-feast
in Lambeth, 1042. His half-brother Eadward the
Confessor reigned in his stead.

6. The Downfall of the Danelaw.

Eadward's reign was disturbed throughout by a
struggle between the Anglo-Scandinavians and the
Franco-Scandinavians.   The king, half Norman by
birth and wholly Norman by training, failed only by
want of energy to make England as Norman as
himself.   On the other side were not merely the
Danish and Norse populations of the Danelaw, but
the family of Godwine, by Knút's favour ruler of
Southern England and the husband of the Danish
lady Gyda, sister to jarl Ulf.   Ulf had married Knút's
sister 'Astrid ; their son Svein, nephew by marriage to
Godwine, was heir to the throne of Svein Forkbeard.
It was only by the promise of succession at Eadward's
death that he was induced to forego his claim upon
England and content himself with the endeavour to
win Denmark, an endeavour in which he succeeded.
His brother Björn became earl of Wessex ; Godwine's

half Danish daughter became queen of England ;
and these examples are only typical of the divided
interests of a realm consisting of half-a-dozen different
territories having no common traditions, and inhabited
by groups of peoples varying in origin, many of them
new-comers, and all of them more concerned with
petty aspirations and animosities than with patriotic
ideals.   We do them wrong if we blame their
blindness.   "England," in the sense we attach to
the word, as the expression of a national unit, did
not exist.

For example, there was nothing to prevent an
"Englishman," now that the trade was learnt, from
turning Viking himself, and playing the pirate on his
native shores.   Osgod Clapa, king's "minister," being
exiled, in 1049 returned with a fleet, part of which
attacked Walton-on-the-Naze.   Svein, the eldest son
of Godwine, at the same time kidnapped and
murdered his cousin Björn of Wessex.   Harold, the
hero of the English, when his family was "under a
cloud," took refuge in Dublin, and in 1052 came back
to ravage Devon, and then, joining his father Godwine,
who had brought a fleet from Flanders, attacked Kent
until the king yielded and reinstated them.   Ælfgar
Leofric's son, Harold's rival, imitated him twice over
(1055 and 1058), regaining his earldom with the help
—first of Irish Danes, and finally with a great fleet of
Norse from the Isles.   But the most characteristic
and unscrupulous of these English Vikings was
Tosti, son of Godwine, whose fatal adventure shook
not only the Danelaw but the whole fabric of Anglo-

Saxon England to its downfall.   A few words will be enough to fix the sequence of events.

Siward the Stout of Northumbria died in 1055; Henry of Huntingdon tells how he would not die "the death of a sick cow," but bade his folk bring helmet and sword and battle-axe, "and when armed according to his desire he gave up the ghost." His earldom did not descend to his son Waltheof, nor to Eadulf's son Oswulf, but to King Eadward's and Queen Eadgyth's favourite Tosti.   But Tosti left his earldom to the care of an underling, and amused himself at court.   When he did interfere with Northumbrian affairs it was for mischief.   Gamel Ormsson and Ulf Dolfinsson were murdered at his house at York; Gospatric was murdered at the Queen's Court— at least folk called it murder, and laid it to Tosti. The Northumbrians rose against him; on October 3, 1065, three of their chief men attacked his house at York, and slaughtered his húskarls.   The names of these Yorkshiremen are not without significance : Gamelbearn, a Norseman, Dunstan son of Æthelnoth, an Englishman, and Glonieorn (Glunier in *Yorks. Domesd.*) son of Heardulf, connected with the royal Danish family of Dublin, for the Gaelic Gluniarainn, translating the Norse Járn-kné, was famous among the O'Ivar; one of the name was half-king in 851, another was father of Ottar jarl, the comrade of Ragnvald who became king of York, and a third was son of Olaf Cuaran.   With these leaders the people of Northumbria deposed Tosti and invited Mórkári, son of Ælfgar, to be their earl.   He led

them south ; at Northampton they were joined by
Eadwine, son of Ælfgar and earl of north-west Mercia,
and they plundered the country, carrying away
captives, until they reached Oxford. In spite of
Harold's mediation and King Eadward's support,
Tosti was forced to leave the country (November 1,
1065).

On January 5, 1066, Eadward the Confessor died,
and next day Harold was crowned king. He was
acknowledged by the Northumbrians only after
his personal appearance among them and on the
appeal of bishop Wulfstan of Worcester, Eadwine and
Mórkári remaining in their earldoms. Tosti meanwhile was planning armed re-entry. In May he came
from Normandy (so Freeman, *Norman Conquest*, iii.,
pp. 720–725) to plunder the Isle of Wight, the south
coast and Lindsey. Driven away from the Danelaw
by Eadwine and Mórkári, he took refuge with King
Malcolm in Scotland. Then he applied to Svein of
Denmark for help to invade England; Svein, his
cousin, could do no more than offer him an earldom
in Denmark. He went to the Vík, where, according
to the saga, he found Harald Hardrádi, and though
the Norwegians are said to have feared the English
húskarls, Tosti persuaded the king of Norway to
join him in attempting the conquest of England.

The haste with which the Norwegian fleet was fitted
out suggests that the preparations made by William
of Normandy were no secret; it was a race for the
English crown. Half the fighting force of Norway
was called together ; and the fleet, *Heimskringla* says,

numbered about two hundred war ships beside
transports and boats. Harald Hardrádi came as if
certain of conquest, bringing his queen, his daughters,
and his son Olaf, beside his treasure, including a mass
of gold which twelve strong youths could hardly carry.
But one thing he forgot to bring with him—the invitation which had assured to others of his race a
welcome from their kindred in England.

In the Orkneys he found this welcome from his
island subjects, with whom he left his queen and
daughters, while he took south among his host the
two young jarls Paul and Erlend. On the Tyne
Tosti met him with a contingent raised in Flanders
and in Scotland; the king of Man also sent help,
with others of the Viking states in Ireland and the
Isles. The great fleet ravaged Cleveland, destroyed
Scarborough, harried Holderness, and sailed up the
Humber and the Ouse to Riccall, where the ships
were left under Olaf, the king's son, Paul and Erlend,
and the bishop of Orkney (probably Thórólf, a Norwegian; Orkney not being at that time under the see
of York). Their advance had been rapid, but by this
time Eadwine and Mórkári had called out the fyrd,
and were marching out of York. The armies met at
Fulford, Wednesday, September 20, and the English
were routed with great slaughter. On the Sunday,
York surrendered, promising to receive Harald
Hardrádi as king, and he on his side is said to have
given hostages equal in number to those he received.
York was not sacked, and the army passed by it
to Stamford Bridge, where hostages for the rest of

Northumbria were to be brought, and perhaps (as
Freeman suggests) a royal manor afforded the chance
of provisions. Next morning, Monday, September 25,
Harold Godwine's son arrived in York with his
dreaded húskarls, rode through the city to Stamford
Bridge, and found the Norse army wholly unprepared.
Part of it was on the nearer side of the river, and
was driven across the stream, while one Northman
held the bridge until he was pierced from beneath
through the chinks of the gangway.   Harald Hardrádi
ran out at the alarm, singing—

> Forth we go in battle array,
> Armourless under the blue blade ;
> Helmets shine, but I wear not mine,
> For all our gear in the ships we've laid.

The battle was a surprise, but the Northmen kept up
the fight throughout the day, not without hope of
victory, as Thjodulf Arnorsson's verses, extemporised
in the thick of the battle and still preserved, make
evident.   When Harald Hardrádi fell, the skald,
standing near him, swore in verse to fight on for the
sake of the gallant lads who were left ; but when all
was over, and the English húskarls were masters of
the field, his lament was not without a touch of
bitterness :—

Our folk have paid a fearsome price, so trapped and ta'en they
  be ;
'Twas ill the rede when Harald bade his hosting sail the sea ;
There's ne'er a man among us but is like to rue the day,
For the good king is gone from us, the king's passed away.

" The same day and the same hour when King

Harald fell, his daughter Mary died " in the Orkneys :
" it is said they had but one life," adds the saga.

Two miles from Riccall, where the ships and all
their gear were laid, a curious relic exists, which must
surely in some way be a monument of the battle.   On
the ancient door of the church at Stillingfleet are
figures wrought in iron after the fashion of early Norse
work ; interlaced plaits in thick wire, dragons, and a
swastika of barbed spear-points (a design to be seen
also at Versaas in Vestrgotland) with two quaint men
and a dragon-headed Viking boat with its rudder
shipped, but mastless and oarless, and its forepart
broken away.   It almost seems intended as a symbol
of the wreck of this enterprise, the last great adventure
of the Vikings in England.

Compared with ˙ Harald Hardrádi's invasion the
landing of troops from Denmark two years later was
of little importance, except as part of a disastrous
movement, the history of which must be sketched
because it leads to the ravaging of Northumbria and
the ultimate rearrangement of population in the north
of England.   In 1068, William had not as yet conquered more than the south, though in so doing he
destroyed the centralising machinery which was the
only connexion between the Scandinavian north and
the old realm of Ælfred's family.   He had appointed
Gospatric as earl of Bernicia, and Merlesvein as sheriff
of Yorkshire, but even this concession to local feeling
—and even the fact that Normans had once been
Northmen, which has sometimes been erroneously
imagined to have had weight with both parties—could

not conciliate Northumbria. In spite of the Norse element which Dr. Jón Stefánsson's analysis of the "Festermen" (p. 165) appears to suggest, the people of Yorkshire and surrounding districts (Cumberland must be left out of England until after the reign of William I.) were pro-Danish and not pro-Norse, as the battle of Fulford proved. Gospatric, Merlesvein, and Archill (Arnkill) the chief landholder—höld, as he would have been called a century earlier—invited -King Svein of Denmark to intervene. Whether they intended Eadgar Ætheling to be placed on the throne, or whether they would have preferred direct relations with Denmark, is doubtful.

At first, the movement seemed to die away with the submission of Eadwine, Mórkári, Archill, and the bishop of Durham, and the flight of Eadgar Ætheling, Gospatric and Merlesvein to Scotland. York and Lincoln received William and gave hostages, among whom was perhaps Thurgod, known later as bishop of St. Andrews and biographer of St. Margaret of Scotland, who escaped from Lincoln Castle, and took ship at Grimsby, to the surprise of certain ambassadors from William to King Olaf when they chanced to find him on board (see the story in Symeon's *Hist. Regum*, *s.a.* 1074). Meanwhile the sons of King Harold of England, who had taken refuge at Dublin, returned with a fleet to attack Bristol and the southwest, as they did again next year, to little purpose. But in 1069, after a fresh rising against the Normans in Durham and York, King Svein at last despatched his promised contingent. The fleet under his brother

Ásbjörn, once an earl in England, attacked Kent and
East Anglia without success; it was not until they
entered the Humber that they met with a welcome.
They were joined by the people, and by Waltheof, son
of the famous Siward and now earl of Northampton.
At York the native townsfolk received them gladly,
and the two Norman castles, together with a great
part of the city, were destroyed after severe fighting.

But when this was done, the English dispersed and
the Danes went back to their ships. There seems to
have been no attempt to establish the independence
of Northumbria; one is led to suppose that jealousies
left them without a leader or a programme. The one
man who had a programme was William. He
advanced slowly northward; wasted Staffordshire,
part of the old Danelaw; attacked the Danes in
Lindsey, forcing them into Holderness; marched by
Pontefract to York, and then effected the great devastation of the north. William next devastated the
county of Durham, the sacred land of St. Cuthbert,
which even the Vikings in their fiercest days had
spared. Then marching against Chester he ravaged
Cheshire, Derbyshire, Staffordshire and Shropshire.
In the winter he bribed Ásbjörn and his Danes to
leave, partly by allowing them to plunder Lindsey
as they pleased. Ten years later the terrible reprisals
of bishop Odo for the murder of bishop Walcher in
Durham added to the desolation; though, after such
a tale, one may ask—what more could be added?
And when in *Domesday* we still find Scandinavian
names among the landholders, and later we still find

Scandinavian characteristics in the north of England,
we cannot but inquire—Is not the account of the
destruction of life overdrawn? or, if not, whence did
the fresh population come? In 1378, for example,
nearly forty of the surnames on the roll of freemen of
York may be derived (according to Dr. Jón Stefánsson in the article quoted above) from Norse nicknames. At this present time the dialect, folklore
and physical characteristics of Yorkshire and Lincolnshire are strongly Scandinavian, almost, if not quite,
as much so as those of Cumberland, in which no
soldier of William the Conqueror ever set foot.

The depopulation was possibly as severe as Freeman makes it, following Symeon of Durham, who had
full local knowledge, but perhaps a tradition of animosity which has somewhat exaggerated the area of
devastation.   Large tracts were entirely ravaged;
other parts escaped.   The mere fact that people
could sell themselves as slaves is enough to show that
there were buyers, kind ladies like Geatflæd, who
took the homeless flock of Gospatric, Danish and
English, under her care, and set them free when
the storm was past.   Many, of course, were not so
fortunate; but many must have found a refuge in
Westmorland and North Lancashire among a kindred
and still independent population; others certainly
fled north into Scotland.

In a paper for the Yorkshire Archæological Society
(*Y. A. J.*, vol. xix., 1906) on the ethnology of West
Yorkshire, by Dr. Beddoe and Mr. J. H. Rowe, the
strong Scandinavian character of the people of south-

eastern Scotland is attributed to immigration (or
rather the captivity of great numbers—see Symeon,
Hist. Regum, s.a. 1070) from the East and North
Ridings in the eleventh century. The "wastes" mentioned in *Domesday*, when plotted on the map, show
that the area of devastation extended from Armley to
Gargrave and from Holmfirth to Adel, including all
Upper Airedale and Upper Calderdale; Upper Teesdale and the districts of Northallerton and Driffield
also suffered. But there were areas of safety around
Conisborough, Elmsall, Sherburn, Beverley and Bedale.
These areas of devastation are not due only to William
the Conqueror; mischief was also caused by the
ravages of Malcolm Canmore; but Dr. Beddoe infers
from the map that William moved at first north and
north-east, destroying the eastern parts of the West
and North Ridings, and nearly all the East Riding
except Beverley. Then crossing the Tees, and finding
the natives prepared for his attack, he moved south
and south-west, crossing the Upper Aire, and so into
Amounderness. Malcolm following him crossed
Stainmoor, ravaged Teesdale, Cleveland and South
Durham; and Odo subsequently ravaged Durham, as
we have noticed. But there was evidently a dis-
crimination in William's ravaging, whether he had a
reason for sparing certain places, like Beverley, or
whether he merely swept the country in his line of
march, without "going into the corners." Of about two
hundred or more landowners in the West Riding mentioned in *Domesday*, most of them with Scandinavian
names, about a quarter survived the devastation;

M

most of the greater landholders outlasted the calami-
ties of nearly twenty years, perhaps taking refuge in
Scotland and returning to make their peace.   The
common people, though agriculture was destroyed,
still were not entirely without resources ; there must
have been sheep, bees, hens, fish, swine and wood
left—means of life not then taxable, and therefore
not mentioned in *Domesday.* . At the same time, the
distress and depopulation, however we minimise it,
was terrible and widespread.

Whence, then, was Yorkshire re-peopled ?   To a
great extent it must have been by immigration from
Cumbria and Westmorland.   All over the west of
Yorkshire are place-names containing " thwaite," and
in situations suggesting more recent settlement than
surrounding hamlets or villages ; these seem to represent the additional land taken up by the new-comers,
who betray their presence by these " thwaites " and
other Norse " test-words," among which may be
reckoned *ergh* and *airy*, *-bergh* (common in Westmorland, but only occasional in Yorkshire), and possibly
force and *gill.*   The close resemblance of Cleveland
characteristics, as described by Canon Atkinson in his
Forty Years in a Moorland Parish, to those of the
Lake District suggests a common origin, reaching back
rather to the eleventh and the twelfth centuries than
to the days of Halfdan.   The East Riding (as Beverley was a sanctuary) perhaps retained much of its
population though the farms were destroyed ; but the
coast, and especially Holderness, had only too frequent
experiences of the kind, and with Lindsey must have
suffered enormously.

Some suggestion of new Norse settlements in Lincolnshire has been already made (p. 112). Still we find eastern Yorkshire and Lincolnshire to be, 800 years later, as they were 300 years earlier, Scandinavian districts. Lancashire, in which the dialect is more akin to that of the Midlands, filled up from the south, except Lonsdale, which is closely related to Westmorland.

Thus the population of Yorkshire, and by its analogy we may conclude the same of the whole Danelaw, underwent great changes during the twelfth century; and the preponderance of Scandinavian blood was further reduced by immigration as the various industries sprang up and invited skilled workmen from distant parts. Not only the Normans but Flemings in the twelfth century, and Germans in the fourteenth, came into the country: the mines at Alston were worked about 1350 by a party from Cologne under Tillmann, and the great German colony under Hechstetter in the time of Elizabeth made a notable addition to the Lake District population. Even in the fourteenth century, as can be seen from the poll-tax returns of Yorkshire, names suggest immigration from various parts of England, from Scotland and Ireland and from France. Consequently the ethnology of Northumbria is no easy problem to unravel, and anything like pure Scandinavian descent is not to be expected. Dr. Beddoe and Mr. Rowe (see the paper above quoted) took measurements in 1902 of twenty men of pure local descent in Oakworth and Haworth, finding types of very different origin in this closely associated group

of samples : two were of the Bronze Age type, six
Anglian, two of von Hölder's Sarmatic, two Scandinavian, probably of Norse origin, and one perhaps
Danish. Of these thirteen less than half could be
distinctly traced to Viking immigration, and this in
a district where the survival of the race must have
been most marked. And yet, in the more remote dales,
where the mixture of blood caused by the influence
of manufacturing centres is smallest, one cannot but
be struck with the general resemblance of the people
to Danes and Norse. In Cumberland, among the
" old stocks " on fell farms, one meets with men—less
frequently with women—whose faces and figures take
one suddenly back to the fell farms of Iceland ; there
is no doubt that the same mixture of Celtic and Norse
blood, and similar occupations and habits of life have
preserved the likeness.

During the twelfth century Scandinavian names of
landowners and others were still common throughout
the old Danelaw, though it became fashionable to give
Norman names to great folk's children, and during
the next century the old Norse names were only kept
up by the lower classes. But even in 1285 and
following years we find, as deerstealers in Inglewood,
the great royal forest of Cumberland (see Mr. F. H.
M. Parker's article in *Trans. Cumb. and West. Antiq.
Soc.*, N.S., vii.), Stephen son of *Gamel*, Henry son of
Hamund, William *Turpyn* (Thorfinnsson), Richard
Siward (the name of Suart is still common) and Hugh
Gowk (*gaukr*, a cuckoo, A.-S. *gēac* shows that " gowk "
is from the Norse ; see Björkman, *Scandinavian Loan-*

words in Middle English ; " Borrowdale gowks " is an
old jest, and see p. 253 for the name of one of the rune-
carvers in the Orkney Maeshowe). These Norse names
were then going out of fashion.   A Cumberland deed
of 1397 .(Mr. W. N. Thompson, *Trans. Cumb. and
West. Ant. Soc.*, N.S., vi.) mentions Richard
Thomson, son of Thomas Johanson, showing the true
patronymic as still used in Iceland : of which the
feminine occurs in Elena Robyndoghter, Magota
Jakdoghter, Matilda and Anabilla Daudoghters who,
with Magota Daudwyfe and Johannes Daudson (David-
son), occur in Yorkshire poll-tax returns.   Many more
examples might be given from Yorkshire and Cumberland.   It has been thought that the termination -son
is a mark of Scandinavian origin : and, without
pressing this too far, it may be said that such surnames
are more common in the old Danelaw than elsewhere.
Many, however, of the derivations attempted for
surnames in popular works are too fanciful to stand.
Fawcett, for example, is a place-name, not from
Forseti the god in the Edda ; Huggin can hardly
represent Odin's raven Hugin, nor Frear the god
Freyr, as gravely stated in a work by a well-known
author of the past generation.   Such wild conjectures
have too often brought the study of Norse origins
into contempt ; and yet we owe much to the earlier
students of the subject, from de Quincey downward,
for venturing into the tangled region, and perhaps we
have not even yet escaped all the illusions of the
forest of error.

III. THE NORSE SETTLEMENTS

So far, we have considered only the Scandinavian immigration from the east—settlers, chiefly Danish, who colonised the shores of the North Sea and penetrated Britain halfway across, or in one part more and in another less than halfway. We have now to deal with the counter current of invasion from the west — of settlers, chiefly Norse, who made homes on the coasts of the Irish Sea. In Northumbria they met the streams from the east, interpenetrated the Danish settlements, and, though late in the history of Scandinavian colonisation, made their way, as we have just seen, across Yorkshire. In Scotland they formed the bulk of Scandinavian element in the population. But all the shores of the Irish Sea, and its continuations north and south, were visited by them and retain traces of their presence. The difficulty in treating the subject as matter of history is great, for there are no sufficiently full and consecutive annals of these regions which lie between England and Ireland ; we get little more than occasional hints, and the evidences of place-names and archæology ; but still it is possible to sketch the general course and extent of the movement. The Viking kingdoms in Ireland cannot be rightly included in a review of Scandinavian Britain, and this omission narrows the range of a subject, already too

extensive, and complicated into (1) the settlements
in Wales, (2) those in Lancashire and Cheshire,
(3) Cumberland and Westmorland, (4) Dumfriesshire
and Galloway, (5) Man and the Isles, and (6) the
Earldom of Orkney, including the neighbouring mainland and the Shetland Isles.   It is not our object to
write the histories of these six or more provinces or
kingdoms, but without some brief reference to the
sequence of events it would be hardly possible to
explain the circumstances of the settlements.

1. WALES.

At the beginning of the Viking Age, Cornwall was
"West Wales," and we have seen how Danes from
Ireland tried to get a footing among the natives, but
were overthrown at the battle of Hengston Down.
From the many occasions on which Vikings attacked
Cornwall, Devon, and the neighbouring shires, it could
be inferred that they left signs of settlement, and it is
no surprise to find a church dedicated to St. Olaf in
Exeter, and another, St. Olave's, at Poughill in Cornwall.   But among the many grave-crosses there are
few which can be said with certainty to be of Scandinavian workmanship.   In Mr. A. G. Langdon's volume
on *Old Cornish Crosses*, Cardynham No. 3, with its
chain-ring pattern, seems to be a tenth-century monument of the Norse type found in Northumbria, and
the Lanivet hogback with the bears presents some
resemblances to the bear-hogbacks of Danish type in

Yorkshire. It is curious to find these evidences of settlement so far inland, with a noteworthy absence of similar monuments at churchyards near the coast. On the coast there are a few names distinctively Scandinavian ; the river Helford (Hellufjörðr ?) is the most conspicuous, and it is here that Charles Kingsley in *Hereward* places his eleventh-century Norse kinglet Alef.

In Devonshire place-names in -beer (*Domesday* -bera) do not represent the Scandinavian *bær* which becomes *by*, but the Anglo-Saxon *bearo*, " grove " (Rev. E. McClure, *Dawn of Day*, March 1908). Scandinavian traces exist in folklore and ethnology. The tall fair Devonshire man is supposed to represent a Norse ancestry, and in Cornwall " a red-haired Dane " is still a term of reproach ; but no recorded colony of importance was formed in West Wales. Some Vikings who settled there emigrated after a time. The Macgillimores of Waterford, though adopting an Irish name, are said to have come from Devonshire with others of their kindred ; and at least they claimed English rights at law.

Out to sea the Scandinavian name of Lund-ey, and as we enter the Bristol Channel Flat-holme and Steepholme, recall the fact that war ships and trading ships of the Northmen found their way to the Severn, and remind us of Bristol's ancient commerce with the Ostmen of Ireland. But as soon as we come to Wales proper we can distinguish many Norse names on the map. Two groups, one centring in the peninsula of Gower and the other in Pembrokeshire,

show more than passing visits of the Northmen to the
country they knew as Bretland, the land of the Britons.
From the Welsh annals and various sources we can
gather the frequency of their incursions, and perhaps
deduce the nature of their settlements.

Their first appearance in Glamorgan, 795, does not
seem to have been followed by any attack until about
838, the time of Hengston Down; and then again
there was peace until 860, when they entered Gower
and were again repulsed. Then Ubbi spent some
time in Pembroke before meeting his fate at the Arx
Cynuit (878). About this time, as Asser the Welsh-
man tells us, King Hemeid of Demetia (S.W. Wales)
"often plundered the monastery and parish of St.
Degui" (St. Davids); we may infer that Welsh
kings, like Irish kings, attacked churchmen. Northmen may have been already settled in that district,
but in this case they are not named as the plunderers.
The next attack was the disastrous raid of Ottar
and Hróald (915), in which St. Davids again suffered,
as well as the diocese of Llandaff and both shores
of the Bristol Channel. Then in 955 we find
a king Siferth among the Welsh princes attesting a
charter of King Eadred, and in 962 " King Sigferth
killed himself, and his body lies at Wimborne."
Florence of Worcester is no doubt wrong in resusci-
tating him to row Eadgar on the Dee in 973, but he is
an historical king, with a Scandinavian name, Sigfrith,
and the fact points to a substantial Viking colony
somewhere in Wales.

By this time we have saga-notices of the fact, which,

though mixed with legendary matter, may have some weight. Egil's Saga in describing the battle of Vínheidi (see p. 133) says that two brothers, Hring and Adils, ruled in Bretland as tributaries of Æthelstan, and on the coming of Olaf of Dublin joined him against the English (937). We cannot identify these with any known persons in British annals, but the settlements in Wales must have originated by their time. In what part of Wales is another question ; we have still to notice the progress of Viking affairs in Anglesey and the north. Again we have the story of Pálnatóki, who some time after the middle of the tenth century went viking from Denmark to Bretland, and there found an old jarl, Stefnir, ruling a district with the help of his foster son, Björn the British. Pálnatóki married Olöf, the jarl's daughter, and then associated himself with Svein, son of Harald Blátönn, afterwards conqueror of England, who seems to have spent part of his youth in Wales. Mr. A. G. Moffat (in the *Saga-book of the Viking Club*, iii., p. 163 *seq.*) attempts to localise the story in Pembroke and Cardigan.

The Scandinavian place-names in the neighbour-·hood of Gower, though not so thick on the map as those of Pembroke, show a marked contrast to the Welsh names farther inland, and can hardly be traced to the Norman conquest ; *e. g.* Swansea, spelt in 1188 "·Sweynsei"; Worm's Head, the promontory of the peninsula (cf. Orm'shead); Esperlone or Esperlond, "the aspen grove "; Burry Holme ; and further east along the coast the Nash (*nes ?*), Barry (*Barrey ?*). To these may be added some names in which the

Scandinavian element is doubtful or less obvious. The
Llanrhidian stone appears to be a kind of hogback
and therefore Norse, as the hogbacks are not Celtic.
From 966 for some twenty-five years it seems that the
Vikings had a troublous time in Glamorganshire, and
though they were invited into the country again in
1031 and 1043 to aid in the internecine quarrels of
the Welsh, they established no state important enough
to figure in history. But of their settlement there can
be little doubt.

Farther west the Viking colony seems present at
Caldy, Ramsey, Swanslake, Barnlake (*lækr?*), Gate-
holm, Milford (*fjord*), Lindsway (*vágr*), Hosguard,
Fishguard, Dale, Stack, Solva, Goodwic, Barry,
etc. Here again, however, there is little in the way
of archæological evidence except the Runes on the
Carew Cross (Pembroke Dock) to favour the idea of a
cultured and Christianised settlement. If the story
of Pálnatóki and Svein be localised in Pembroke, we
understand the reason ; for these were of the type of
Vikings who stuck to the old habits. From Caradoc
of Llancarvan we gather that there was no quiet time
in Pembroke. In 981 Godfrid son of Harald (p. 228)
spoiled St. Davids ; in 987 the Danes destroyed
St. Davids and other churches, and forced prince
Meredith to pay the tribute of the Black Army
(Dubhgaill); in 989 they ravaged St. Davids, Cardigan and Kidwely, and were bought off ; in 995
they not only plundered St. Davids but killed—and
the Welsh said ate—the bishop. About 1000–1015
jarl Einar went on frequent voyages to Bretland

from the Orkneys ; and, after the battle of Clontarf,
Flosi the Icelander (*Njáls saga*, clvi., *seq.*) took refuge
in Wales, where he was followed by Kárl Sölmundarson, who twenty years earlier had played the
viking in these parts, and now sought vengeance on
Flosi for the burning of Njál. In some town not
named Kol Thorsteinsson, one of the men who had
murdered Njál in Iceland, was making a home for
himself, marketing and courting a lady, with the
intent to marry her and settle down.   Kári came into
the town and caught him in the act of counting out
his money, and struck off his head—"and the head
counted 'ten' as it flew from his body."   Whether
this incident so vividly told happened in Conway or
Chester, Milford or Swansea, we cannot guess, but
we can see that the Northmen were at home in Wales,
in spite of their turbulent dealings with neighbours
not far away ; and whatever legend may be involved,
the story adds to the evidence of a definite
settlement.

   That the Vikings in Ireland were in constant
communication with the coast of Wales is abundantly
proved.   In 1041 King Gruffydd was captured by
Norse from Dublin (Caradoc), and Guttorm with King
Murchadh ravaged Wales; but in 1049 the same
Irish-Norse or their near kindred joined Gruffydd in an
attack on the Severn (Florence).   After this the Vikings
seem to have been used as convenient tools for any
discontented party—English ealdormen in exile, or
Welsh princes in defeat—but their existence in Wales
remained a settled fact.   And yet the colony in

Pembroke was never, like the Cumbrian colony, extended far inland. Its operations appear to cover the country surrounding the great fjord which give a haven to Viking ships. Many of the place-names which have tempted etymologists to doubtful conclusions must have resulted from the English settlement under the Norman rule. The Northmen seem to have occupied only the central and southern part of the country, and to have used the place as a factory or emporium—a stronghold for piracy and a centre of slave traffic—where the worse traditions of the Viking Age survived ; not making it, as in other parts of Britain, an area of peaceful colonisation and steady domestic progress.

Much the same story must be told of North Wales. We have noticed the invasion of Orm in 855, and the history of the coast from Anglesey to Chester is one tale of repeated attacks rather than permanent settlement. In 873, according to Caradoc of Llancarvan, Danes landed in Anglesey, and were driven off in two battles by Roderic; in 878 Roderic's death was revenged by the battle of Cymrhyd, near Conway. Then followed more Danish attacks on the north Welsh coast, until, in 900, Igmund or Ingimund from Dublin with his Norse landed at Holyhead and fought their way to Chester, after which they found homes in Wirral. Then, in 909, the Danes from Dublin, who had driven out these Norse, followed them, and besieged Chester, lately fortified by the English. About 920, as Caradoc and William of Malmesbury say, Leofred from Dublin joined Gruffydd ap

Madoc to attack Chester again (if this is not the same story twice told).

In 961 the sons of Olaf Cuaran of Dublin (or Olaf's son and the Lagmen of the Islands) are said to have landed in Anglesey and burnt Holyhead. In 966 another attack is recorded, and in 969 Mactus (Magnus) Haraldsson, of the Isle of Man, entered Anglesey and spoiled Penmon, but was driven out in 970. In 979 a Welsh faction hired Danes under Godfrid, son of Harald, king of Man, to invade Anglesey, and in 986 Godfrid came again, took Llywarch ap Owain prisoner with 2,000 men, and put Meredith ap Owain to flight. In 991 the Danes once more overran the island. In 993 Svein Forkbeard landed in North Wales from the Isle of Man. Then we come, as before, to the period when race counted for little, and the Vikings were used as tools of faction. Conan, son of Iago ap Idwal, in 1041 taking refuge in Ireland and marrying the daughter of the king of Dublin, returned to North Wales and captured prince Gruffydd. In 1056 Roderic, son of Harald, "king of Denmark," came to Wales, joined Gruffydd and invaded England ; in 1073 Gruffydd, son of Conan, got help in Ireland from the king of Ulster and "Ranallt" and other kings to invade Anglesey, as he did again in 1079. At last came Magnus of Norway in 1096 and 1100, to whom Anglesey was the southernmost goal in his career of belated and fruitless viking. (See Caradoc, 961–1100.)

The story of these repeated incursions leads one to expect some permanent colonisation in North Wales. The Viking character is expressed, in spite of the natural animosity which is shown, in Gruffydd's confirmation of lands to bishop Herwald of Llandaff (1032–1061), when he promises to defend the Church against the "barbaros Anglos," and the Irish of the west, "semper fugaces," the Danes of the sea and the inhabitants of the Orkneys, "semper versis dorsis in fugam et firmato fœdere ad libitum suum pacificatos" (Clark's *Cartæ et Munimenta*, iii., 30, quoted by Mr. A. G. Moffat).

Scandinavian relics in North Wales are few. Of place-names beside Anglesey and Orm's Head, there are Priestholme (Puffin Island), the Stacks (Holyhead), the Skerries (N.W. of Anglesey), Bardsea, perhaps the island home of a Viking named Bard, and the Point of Air (*eyrr*) at the mouth of the Dee. But such a name as Wig, between Bangor and Aber, may be from the Welsh *gwig*, "nemus," not from *wic*, nor from *vik*, and it must be owned that most derivations of North Welsh names from the Norse are not very satisfactory. In Penmon Priory is said to be a cross of Swedish type ; and the Maen-y-chwynfan in Flintshire has a strong likeness to tenth-century crosses in Cumberland, and must be a relic of Christianised Viking settlement. But here we are on the border of a country where such settlement has left more plentiful traces than in North Wales.

2. CHESHIRE AND LANCASHIRE.

In the year 900 Æthelflæd, Lady of the Mercians, granted to Ingimund expelled from Dublin certain wasted lands near Chester, where Hástein had been ravaging (*Caradoc* and *Three Fragments*). This dates the Norse settlement near the mouth of the Dee, both on the Flintshire side and in Wirral, the peninsula between the Dee and the Mersey. The colony has a peculiar interest from the fact that its Thingwall (in *Domesday* Tingvelle, *Thingvellir*), is preserved to us, at least in name. The so-called Thor's Stone near Thurstaston (*Domesday* Turstanetone, Thórsteins tún), - a terraced rock-mound with a flat summit, looks like a Thingmount, but there is no reason to believe that it is other than a rather curious natural development of the local red sandstone. On the other hand, there are several monuments which must be referred to this tenth-century Norse colony. The hogback in the museum at West Kirby, though it cannot have come from Ireland as tradition says, is like the work of Vikings of that century who did come from Ireland to Cumbria. A wheel-head grave-slab in the same museum, and the similar stone at Hilbre Island, look like early works of the period. At Neston are fragments of cross-shafts of the Anglo-Norse type, and the Bromborough cross appears to be, like similar monuments in the Grosvenor Museum and in St. John's Church, Chester, of late tenth-century date.

Many of the place-names of Wirral are Norse in form. This would naturally be the case where waste lands were taken by new settlers; though as estates were held under Mercia, and not as a free and independent colony, it is hardly surprising to find that the Danish system of land-assessment was not used here

at the period of *Domesday*. Beside the names already
mentioned we may note Raby, Irby, Pensby, Helsby
Frankby, and Whitby ; Greasby is Gravesberia in
Domesday, but Signeby is named there ; Noctŏrum
in *Domesday* Chenoterie, but in the thirteenth century
Knocttyrum, perhaps from the Celtic *cnoc*, " hill," or
from Hnotar-holm, nut-field, as -holm often becomes
-um in terminations ; Tranmere, *Tranmull*, crane's
ness ; Hoylake (*lœkr*) ; Meols (*melar*) ; Landican, in
Domesday Landechene, possibly Lann-Aedhagain, the
chapel of Athacan, a Gaelic name used by the writers
of Norse runes in the Isle of Man. A similar Celtic
importation may be Poole (*Domesday*, Pol), for the
Irish Norse must have brought Celtic words to Wirral,
as they did to Cumberland (see *Saga-book of Viking
Club*, ii., pp. 141–147).

But the chief interest of the names in Wirral is the
evidence they give of the system of Norse settlement
on uninhabited country, precisely the same as in
Iceland. We can see that each head of a household
received a slice of land with a frontage to the fjord of
Mersey or of Dee—in which the most southern creek
is Shotwick, *Domesday* Sotowiche (*Suðrvík ?*). The
estate reached inland up to the less cultivable high
ground. In each landtake the *bóndi* fixed his homestead, neither on the exposed hilltop nor on the
marshy flat. He made his *bœr*, a group of buildings,
in the *tún*, or homefield, which he manured and
mowed for hay, and surrounded with a garth. Thurstaston, Thorstein's *tún*, must have been a Norse
farm, though Bebbington was a surviving name from

N

the Anglian Bebbingas who may have held it before Hástein's time. A place called Brimstage, anciently Brunstath (but not a "staithe") or Brynston, shows that *staðr* and *tún* were convertible terms, "Well-stead," or "Well-ton." Storeton may be Stór-tún, "big field," or the first element may be from *storð*, "coppice," as in Storth, Stotthes and Storrs in the Lake District. Oxton lying on the saddle of a long ridge (*ok*), must be *Oks-tún*, "the farm on the yoke," grammatically named. As time went on, secondary settlements must have been formed, as we saw in Lincolnshire. The younger sons of a *bóndi*, or his freedmen, would receive bits of less valuable ground inland. A name like Irby, though in Yorkshire perhaps derived from a settler Ivar, might be *Ira-bœr*, the farm of the Irishmen, perhaps dependents of the owner of Thorstein's *tún*, above which it lies. Raby (similar names occur in Cumberland, Isle of Man, Lancashire and Denmark,) means a farm on the boundary of, or wedged in between, two greater estates.

Around these farmsteads were the acres where they sowed "big and barr," and the pastures recognised by -well and -wall, as Crabwall, *Krapp-völlr*, "narrow field"; Thingwall, as already noted, *Thing-vellir*, "parliament fields." Each estate had its woods, such as Birket (*birk-with*), for fuel, and the termination -grave may mean charcoal-pits or turbaries for peat (*cf.* Kolgrafafjord, Iceland, as well as A.-S. *gráf*, "grove"). A field that slopes from a hill to a swamp is called in Iceland *thveit ;* the word "thwaite" in the Lake District denotes more than a mere clearing or cut-off place, and

usually is associated with ancient sloping pasture-land.
In Wallasey there are fields called thwaites, testifying to
the Norse origin of the agricultural system at the time
when these names were given.   The *hólmr*, *kjarr*
(carr) and *mýrr* served, before the days of drained
land, as they do in Iceland now, for pasturing larger
cattle ; lambs and calves were herded on the higher
ground.   The name Calday (*Domesday* Calders) near
Thurstaston, perhaps meant "calf-dales," as Calgarth
at Windermere was anciently Calv-garth, and Calder
in Caithness was Kalfadalsá.   Sheep were sent up the
moor by the Rake (from *reka*, to drive), and we find
the name at Eastham, as well as in Scotland and
north England.   In summer the cattle were pastured
on the moor, and the dairymaids had their sæters or
shielings, which when the land became more cut up
into smaller holdings became independent farms ;
hence the names containing satter and seat in the
Lake District, sometimes dropping the last consonant
and producing Seathwaite, Seascale.   In Wirral, Sea-
combe appears to represent the *hvammr* or "combe
of the seat," or sæter.   Other words to express the
same practice are of the type of Summerhill and Sella-
field, found in the north of England, and also the
borrowed Gaelic *airidh* or *ergh*, found in the Orkneys
and Hebrides, as well as throughout Northumbria and
Galloway in various forms.   Here in Wirral we find it
as Arrow, parallel with the same name at Coniston, and
perhaps giving us the *sæter* of the Gallgael Norseman
who had his *bær* at Thurstaston.

In the middle of the peninsula where the moorland

pastures of the first settlers met, is Thingwall ; and near it is Landican, which, if we are right in explaining the name as the chapel of an Irish saint or priest, stands in relation to the Thingstead as the central church in the Isle of Man does to the Tynwald. And further, we see that Ingimund's Norse were already Christian-ised in Dublin and brought their religion with them ; or, if they were not all as yet Christians, we may be sure that the Lady of the Mercians insisted that settlers under her rule should be baptised, though she did not make them take an English priest. But just up the hillside, above the muddy dell in which the chapel stood, is Prenton (in *Domesday*, Prestune), the priest's farm. As in Iceland, the priest farmed his own glebe. Later, when a new church was built, perhaps (from its monuments) a generation or two after the first settlement, the farm attached to it was known as *West* Kirk-by. The churches at Neston and Bromborough, as the crosses suggest, are of the end of the tenth century, or early in the eleventh. Overchurch, of course, was pre-Viking, and no doubt destroyed by Hástein, or even earlier.

In Wirral we seem to have the first of those agricul-tural settlements which characterise the Norse of the west coast, as distinguished from the predatory and trading centres of the Vikings in Wales, and the con-quered lands of the great Danish invasion in the east of England. To their presence in Cheshire must have been due the rise of the town refounded by ealdorman Æthelred, for its wealth in the eleventh century was won by trade with Dublin (see Mr.

Round's *Feudal England*, p. 465), and the Scandinavian character of Chester is shown by the fact that it was ruled by "lawmen," as were the Five Boroughs.

A second Norse colony, of which we have no historical record, must have existed north of the Mersey. Thingwall, east of Liverpool, would be a convenient centre for a number of places with names such as Roby, (West) Derby, Kirkby, Crosby, Formby, Kirkdale, Toxteth (Stockestede in *Domesday*) and Croxteth (not *staithes*, being inland), Childwall (Cildeuuelle, *Kelduvellir*), Diglake, Harbreck, Ravensmeols, Ormskirk, Altcar (Acrer), Carrside, Cunscough (*Skógr*), Skelmersdale (Schelmeresdele, *Skálmýrrsdalr*). Of forty-five place-names in West Derby Hundred mentioned in *Domesday*, five are Anglo-Saxon and ten are Scandinavian; the rest might be interpreted in either dialect. In the remainder of South Lancashire all the names in *Domesday* are Anglo-Saxon, but there are only twelve altogether, for the land was partly waste at the time and partly free from assessment. Hence, when we look at the map, we can recognise a great number of Norse names which do not appear in *Domesday* : some, no doubt, were later settlements and owe their Scandinavian form to the persistence of the dialect, but many must be original. Of the persons named in the survey, three of the landowners in West Derby have Scandinavian names ; three more are probably Scandinavian, whilst seven are Anglo-Saxon. In Warrington six "drengs" have Norman names, and one Scandinavian ; but the word "dreng" itself is Scandinavian, and the tenure indicates the survival of old relations

other than those of Saxon England. South Lancashire formed a part of Cheshire after the break-up of
the Danish kingdom of York; in 1002 the will of
Wulfric Spot, founder of the abbey of Burton-upon-
Trent, mentions his great possessions in Wirral and
the land between Mersey and Ribble; so that the
bœndr here held by Mercian rules, although, as
noticed on p. 122, it is possible that the hides and
hundreds of this district really replaced a previous
system of division analogous to that of the Danelaw.

The Winwick crosshead is remarkable evidence of
imported Celtic art of the late tenth century, probably
indicating the presence of a sculptor from the Hebrides,
if not a family of Hebridean origin. As the chroniclers
tell us that in 980 Northern or Hebridean pirates
invaded Cheshire, it is possible that this gives the
occasion for the introduction of the person who
carved this work; but by the analogy of Viking
settlements elsewhere it is evident that there was
continual movement. It was part of every young
man's education, so to speak, to travel either as a
pirate or a merchant, or both; and intercourse with
distant Scandinavian lands was the normal order of
life. The Barton fragment seems to be a tenth
century work with Viking ring-plaits; and these
monuments of South Lancashire and West Cheshire
contrast strongly with the group of Mercian round-
shafted crosses in the east of Cheshire, and no less
strongly with the Northumbrian pre-Viking crosses of
Bolton, Whalley and in North Lancashire. The
distribution of monuments adds to the force of the

remark that many Norse-sounding place-names of
East Lancashire may have been given to places
settled at a much later date than the colonies of
Wirral and the Liverpool district.

In Amounderness, the Agemundrenesse of *Domesday*, the land between Ribble and Morecambe Bay,
we find a third Scandinavian colony, which has
given the name to the district—*Ogmundar-nes.* It is
unlikely that Ögmund was the Ingimund of 900, for
this territory was hardly within the gift of Æthelflæd
of Mercia. The fact that at Heysham on Morecambe
Bay there is a " bear hogback " of the Yorkshire type
does not prove, as might seem at first sight, that the
colony came from Danish Yorkshire by way of
Craven ; for this hogback must be of the very end of
the tenth century, and if the gift of the district by
Æthelstan to St. Peter at York in 930 be genuine,
the name must have been already in use. Indeed,
when we remember that the rest of the seaboard of
Lancashire was colonised early in that century, it is
difficult to believe that this one part remained
unoccupied. Here, again, *Domesday* gives us some
data. Of fifty-eight place-names only twenty appear
to be distinctly Anglo-Saxon or otherwise earlier than
the Viking invasion ; eight are distinctly Scandinavian,
including two in *-argh*, meaning a Norse sæter ; and
the rest are possibly Scandinavian, though they might
be interpreted as Anglian. In the neighbouring
district of Lonsdale about twelve *Domesday* place-
names seem to be Anglo-Saxon, eight Scandinavian
and twenty-eight doubtful. In Furness and South

Cumberland twenty-eight names are given, of which half-a-dozen are Anglo-Saxon, three or four distinctly Norse or Danish, and the rest indeterminate. But of the landowners in North Lancashire mentioned in *Domesday*, all have Scandinavian names except two which are Celtic; probably their families were of Irish-Viking or Gallgael origin.

The monuments tell the same tale. There are at Lancaster and round about many fine Anglian sculptures, showing refinement and wealth in the eighth and ninth centuries; but with these are as many of the Viking Age, proving that the tenth century new-comers were Christian, or soon became so, and carved tombstones in a style which indicates their own native taste influenced by their association with Ireland. The area of these remains reaches from Melling up the Lune Valley to Heysham on the coast, but does not— so far as our knowledge goes at present—extend to the southern parts of Amounderness, where it is to be supposed there was less wealth and culture. It is chiefly at the seaports and centres of travel, on the great highways of commerce, that such works of art are found. The Melling stone is interesting as bearing the same pattern with similar monuments in Norse parts of Cumbria and Scotland, though not Celtic like the Winwick cross. The cross at Halton, further down the Lune, has panels representing the story of Sigurd the Völsung, a work of the eleventh century. The Lancaster Hart and Hound cross is a remarkable example of Norse art with Celtic influences; but the most noteworthy of the series is the "hogback" at

Heysham, upon which figures are sculptured which seem
to represent a kind of illustration of the " Völuspá,"
that poem of the Edda which the editors of the *Corpus
Poeticum Boreale* date about A.D. 1000 or a little
earlier—the heathen forecast of the Day of Doom
which the Christian world expected in that year.
The artist of this work, if he can be called an artist,
must have come from Yorkshire, but the poem no
doubt came from the Hebrides ; and the later years
of the tenth century fit the time when such work
could be imagined and executed. So we get a hint
of the life and belief on the shores of Morecambe
Bay when the colony was already well established,
rich enough to afford such monuments, Christianised
enough to recognise their meaning, and yet clinging
to the old associations and in touch by traffic and
peaceful intercourse with heathen kindred over-seas.

One more monument of the North Lancashire
group must be noticed as showing how long this
Norse colony lasted, using its old language and, in
spite of the Norman Conquest and all that the organisation of the twelfth century meant, clinging to its
individuality. At Pennington in Furness is a Norman
tympanum of a church built about the middle of the
twelfth century, carved by " Hubert the mason " but
built under the patronage of Gamel de Pennington,
a descendant of the old Viking landholders of the
place. The inscription is in Scandinavian runes,
and the language is a clipped Norse, not yet passed
into English :—" (Ga)mial seti thesa kirk ; Hubert
masun van . . ." So we have documents in stone,

in the absence of written records, giving the area and duration of these three Norse colonies between Cambria and Cumbria.

3. CUMBERLAND AND WESTMORLAND.

It is hardly possible to draw any boundary line between the Viking areas round Morecambe Bay and those of Cumbria. In ancient times the sands joined opposite coasts of these great bays and estuaries, where the ordinary map, coloured blue to high-water mark, suggests deep sea : the mountains were the real "scientific frontier," and thus it happened that the south of the Lake District was naturally associated with Lancaster and dissociated from Cumberland in a manner which seems strange to one who knows England only from the map. But the mountain country seems to have been gradually filled up with Norse farming-settlements, and though perhaps the earliest Viking immigrants of Cumbria clustered together on the west coast, forming a group like those of Wirral, South Lancashire and Amounderness, and possibly also Furness, yet it cannot have been long before all the available lands were occupied. How completely this was the case is seen in the place-names. There are certain survivals of the Anglian settlement which followed the Roman roads, coming north and west from Manchester and Leeds to Lancaster, and thence up the Lune and Kent and across the sands to Furness ; also coming over Stainmoor and down the Eden to Carlisle, thence round the coast to Ellenborough and Ravenglass; and thirdly, by way of the Roman Wall to Bewcastle and Irthington. But these Anglian sites are all in the lowlands; in the mountain country the ancient names are Norse, overlying a few Celtic survivals.

It does not follow that these names of Norse form date from the beginning of the settlement in every case. Some of them are certainly of the twelfth century. Allonby, Aglionby, Gamblesby, Glassonby, Upperby, and still more obviously Isaacby and Parsonby show that the termination -by was applied at a comparatively late date, simply because it was the local word. Allerby is named from Aylward in the eleventh century; Gilsland from Gilles son of Bueth; Sunnygill, written Sunnivegile about 1239, may be referred to a Sunnif whose son Robert is mentioned about 1175. Waberthwaite, Langwathby (twelfth century Langwaldeofby), and Thursby may be named from Wyberth, Waltheof and Thore (Thórir), father of the "Thorfynn mac Thore," to whom Gospatric's charter gave lands acquired by Thórir in the days of jarl Sigurd (earl Siward), who died 1055. This deed (printed *Scot. Hist. Rev.*, i.) shows us also that by then the place-names were Norse: Alnerdall, the dale of the Ellen or Alne with a Norse genitive in -er; bek Troyte ("Troutbeck," now the Wisa) and Caldebek show long-established Norse topography, though in the midst of "lands that were Welsh"—*on eallun þam landann þeo weoron Cõmbres*,"—Cymric, Cumbrian, in which the very villages granted to Thorfinn were

" Cardeu and Combedeyfoch " (Cumdivock). The
use of the word " beck " for a stream in Scandinavian
districts and in combination with words of distinctly
Scandinavian origin is itself a proof of early settlement, before the age of the colonisation of Iceland,
where the word is not unknown (as Kvíabekkr in
Landnáma) but is usually replaced by *Lækr*. In
Icelandic poetry the word *bekkr* was preserved, as
many archaic words survive in verse ; showing that it
was not merely the Danish "test-word" which it has
been supposed to be : and this suggests that the
language of those who gave Cumbrian as well as
Northumbrian place-names must be earlier than
tenth-century Icelandic : a fact which has been already
(p. 56) noted of Shetland.

The monuments also favour this view of an early
settlement.   In Cumberland there are many pre-
Norman grave-stones which belong to the series of
Anglian works carved throughout Northumbria, to
which Cumberland belonged under the great kings of
the seventh and eighth centuries.   Of these the cross-
heads at Carlisle can be traced to a school of art
centering in Northallerton ; obviously this style came
in along the Roman road over Stainmoor : and all
along that road as far as the coast near the great
ancient ports of Ellenborough, Workington and
Ravenglass these Anglian monuments can be seen.
But these are quite as obviously imitated in a series
of crosses which glide into works with distinctly
Norse motives and occasional Irish characteristics, in
the boss-and-spine cross-heads with scroll-work be-

coming worm-twist, and animal forms becoming Scandinavian dragons, and bearing the *swastika* and other symbols not used by the Anglians. This series is followed, late in the tenth century, by another of more advanced skill in carving, such as we have seen must have been developed in Northumbria under Mercian influence after the fall of the independent Viking monarchy—the round-shafted crosses of Northamptonshire and Cheshire, imitated in Yorkshire and then travelling north by the same great route to Penrith and Gosforth, and turning into distinctly Norse forms with illustrations from the Edda poems, such as we have noticed (p. 201) on the Heysham "hogback."

This continuous development from the models found at Carlisle is not likely to have been the work of Halfdan's Danes, who in 875 came there only to plunder and destroy. Their successors, however, who shared in the distribution of lands and settled in the Anglicised parts of Cumberland may have become converted under Guthred and so led to imitate the monuments of the burnt priory, and no doubt the natives, who would be employed as carvers, knew them well. But as we go west from Carlisle we find more and more Scandinavian and Irish elements in the art of the period, so that a somewhat sharp distinction can be drawn between the Anglo-Danish stones of the Yorkshire type and those of West Cumberland ; and we are led to conclude that the bulk of the Cumbrian Vikings were of a different race from the Danes of Northumbria, akin rather to the Norse of Man, Galloway, Ireland and the Hebrides. And the monuments suggest these Norse were already a strong colony in the earlier part of the tenth century.

Of pre-Christian relics of the Vikings in these parts a few examples remain. The Ormside cup, now in the York Museum, seems to be a Viking's loot, carried over Stainmoor from some church in Yorkshire to the spot in the Eden Valley where the early invader made his home—at Ormside (*Orms-setr*), perhaps keeping his very name. In the churchyard has been found a grave-hoard of weapons, evidently an early interment of the days when half-converted heathen were. buried with the grave-goods of the pagan rite, as at Birka, near Stockholm, tenth-century Christians were interred with their personal belongings. Earlier still is the "find" at the tumulus of Hesket-in-the-Forest, near Carlisle, where a sword, bent and broken, as in heathen burials, was found with various weapons and the spur and snaffle of the warrior's horse. Other Viking swords have been found at Workington and Witherslack, the former likewise bent up and broken in its sheath. But down the Eden from Ormside, at Kirkoswald, a trefoil fibula (British Museum), bearing ornament resembling that of a bead of Danish make in the Copenhagen Museum, was found along with coins dating 769–854, or twenty years before Halfdan attacked Carlisle. This seems to mean that Danish Vikings were in the Eden Valley before the date at which chroniclers record their presence. As examples of metal-work coming into Cumbria from the opposite direction, brought in by Norse from the west, may be mentioned the Brayton fibula, perhaps

Irish-Viking in origin, the Orton Scar penannular
fibula, now possessed by the Society of Antiquaries;
the two great "thistle" fibulæ from the neighbourhood of Penrith, now in the British Museum, and a
third, of great size but without the thistle ornament,
found near Kirkby Lonsdale and owned by the
Bishop of Barrow. All these seem to be relics of
the Norse occupation of the tenth century, to which
date they may be referred.

We have noticed the conquest of Strathclyde by
Olaf the White and Ivar "the Boneless" in 870, and
seen that in 875–880 the bearers of St. Cuthbert's
relics could travel in Cumberland and Galloway without hindrance, though driven from Northumberland
by heathen Danes. By that time, however, Norse
from Ireland must have already begun to settle in
Galloway, and possibly in Cumberland, though perhaps in small numbers, and already under the influence of Irish Christianity. It was about or soon
after the close of the pilgrimage of Eardwulf and
Eadred Lulisc that, according to the sagas, Harald
Fairhair invaded the Hebrides and Man. "He came
first by Shetland, and slew there all the Vikings who
fled not from under him. Thence sailed Harald the
king south to the Orkneys and cleared them all of
Vikings. After that he went throughout the Hebrides
and harried there; he slew there many Vikings who
ruled over hosts erewhile. He fought many battles
and always won them. Then he harried in Scotland
and fought battles there. But when he came west to
Man, there they had already heard what harrying he

had done, and all folk fled into Scotland and the
island was left unpeopled: all goods that might be
were shifted and flitted away. So when Harald's men
landed there they took no booty."—(*Heimskringla*,
Harald Fairhair, xxii.) Now. after Halfdan's invasion Cumberland ceased to be Northumbrian.
Early in the tenth century we find it, under native
Welsh kings, as part of Strathclyde, a kingdom
closely connected with Scotland and ultimately, if not
at first, held by the tanist to the Scottish crown. On
this occasion the fugitives from Man could not have
fled in the direction from which their enemy was
coming, and the conclusion is that they emigrated
in mass to the fjords of Solway and Duddon,
and to the hills visible to them from their home in
Man.

The notice in the chronicles that Hástein, after
leaving Chester (895), ravaged the North Welsh, or
North British, applies to what we still call North
·Wales. There was no need for him to go to Cumbria,
in his starving condition, to find food; and the
suggestion that his Danes colonised Cumbria at that
time need not be considered. But less than twenty
years later, if there is any truth in the stories told
by the *Historia de S. Cuthberto* (see p. 128), Vikings
were pressing the Angles of Cumberland, and making
them take refuge eastward, over the fells. In 918 Ottar
and Ragnvald marched through to Corbridge ; indeed,
Ragnvald was known as " Dux Galwalensium," though
this was hardly a territorial title ; he was not the jarl of
Galloway, but the leader of the Gallgael. In 924, not

only the Danes of Northumbria, but the *Northmen* (of this coast) submitted to Eadward, and in 926 the kings of Scotland and Strathclyde met Æthelstan at Dacre, which must have been the Cumberland Dacre, outside Northumbria, but not far within the boundary of the Cumbrian kingdom. It is usual in historical maps to draw a hard and fast line along the Derwent as the southern limit of this mysterious realm, assuming that the later bishopric represented the old kingdom ; but the whole of the mountainous Lake District must have been at this period practically a wilderness. A line of road went through it from Penrith by way of Keswick, near which St. Herbert had his hermitage in the wilds ; but the old Roman route through Ambleside and Hardknott shows no traces of Anglian habitation, and the central moors of Westmorland (Westmoringaland, compare Vestrmæri in Norway, " land of folk of the western meer," or boundary, not of western " meres," nor the Guasmoric of Nennius, 42, nor the realm of Geoffrey's Marius) must have been equally uncivilised until the overflow of Norse settlement filled them with population. The interests of the Strathclyde king were in the north ; his capital was on the Clyde, and Cumberland, though still Cymric, was a no-man's-land.

Through this region, again, Owain of Strathclyde and Constantine's army must have marched to Brunanburh, possibly joined by the Vikings settled here ; for while there were no reprisals made upon the Danelaw for participation in that attack, in 945 king Eadmund " ravaged all Cumberland and granted

O

it to Malcolm, king of the Scots, on condition that he should be his fellow-worker, as well by sea as by land." This can only mean that Domhnall, son of Owain, king of Strathclyde, was permitting the Vikings who were settled there more freedom than the old agreements allowed, and that Eadmund wished, in modern language, to preserve the integrity of a buffer State, through which the enemies of southern England were continually travelling between York and Ireland. An example of this occurs at the time of the battle of Stainmoor (954?), when Eirík, late of York, but since then in the Hebrides and at Waterford, returned to recover his Northumbrian kingdom. Magnus Olafsson (Maccus filius Onlafi) had probably been dispossessed of Man and the Islands. (Professor A. Bugge remarks, in *Caithreim Ceallachain Caisil*, p. 148, that Eirík is called "king of the Hebrides," as confederate of Sigtrygg of Dublin, about the year 953.) Magnus was, perhaps, warned by Oswulf of Bamborough, and invited to join in the attack on Eirík and the five kings from Orkney and Ireland; this may be the meaning of the "treachery" of Oswulf (Roger of Wendover, A.D. 950). But we see Cumberland and Westmorland now in the hands of conflicting parties of Vikings, and can understand why in 966 Thord Gunnarsson, the Danish "minister" of the Saxon king, was deputed to lead a punitive expedition into Westmorland, and why, in 1000, king Æthelred himself attempted once more the reduction of Cumberland.

In spite of these ravagings of Cumberland and

Westmorland, and the fact that armies from time to time marched through the country, there is singularly little to show in the way of fortifications which can be attributed to the period. The Norse settlers did not come as conquerors, entrenching themselves against the natives, but as immigrants seeking a livelihood. The negative evidence from the absence of forts is supported by positive evidence of place-names and dialect survivals. There are a few places in which the already existing fortress is noticed in the name, as the Borrowdales in Cumberland and Westmorland (Borcheredale, in mediæval spelling, *i.e.* Borgar-dalr), the Broughtons (that in Furness apparently the Borch of *Domesday*), Brough-under-Stainmoor (twelfth century Burc) and Burgh-by-Sands, and there is one place near Windermere called Orrest (*Orrösta*), *i.e.* the battle. But the Norse place-names relate almost entirely to farming life or the natural features of the country, except where they preserve a settler's name. Of this latter class are Osmotherley (Ásmundar-ljá) ; Arnside (Arna-sætr) ; Ambleside (Hamel-side or Amel-sate in the thirteenth century) ; Arkleby (Arnkell's bær) ; Bardsey (Berretseige, *Domesday ;* Barröd'segg, edge) ; Burneside (Bronolves-hefd or -helvd ; Brynjólf's "claim"? or "share"?) ; Crosby Ravensworth (Raven's-waite or thwaite, twelfth century) ; Eaglesfield (Eglesfield in *Distributio Cumb.*, Egil's) ; Fins-thwaite ; Godderthwaite (Godröd's) ; Gunnerkeld (Gunnar's) ; Hawkshead (Hawkenside, Haukensehead, Hákon's sætr or "claim") ; Hornsby in Cumwhitton (Ormes-by in 1230) ; Kirkby Stephen and Kirkby Thore (Thórir); Langley (Langlíf's-ergh); Lazenby (farm of the leysingi or freedman); Mansergh (the slave's shieling); Melkinthorpe and Melmerby (from the Irish Maelchon and Maelmor); Ninesergh (Ninian's, in the estates of the ancestors of Gospatric f. Orme); Oddendale (Audun's, not Odin's); Ormside (Orm's sæter); Ousby (about 1240 Ulvesby, Ulf's); Ravenstonedale (the dale of Hrafn's tún); Ramsey (as in Wales and the Isle of Man, etc., Hrafn's island); Renwick (about 1177 written Ravenswic); Rusland (in the thirteenth century Rolesland, Hrólf's); Sizergh (anciently Sigarith-erge); Soulby (perhaps Sölva-bær); Stephney and Stavenerge (West Cumberland, Stephen's or Stefnir's; perhaps not Pálnatóki's father-in-law, p. 186, and yet Cumbria too was Bretland); Swinside (near Flimby, Suanesete, *temp*. Henry II., the sæter of Svein); Thirlmere (perhaps Thorolf's); Thurston-water, *i.e.* Coniston Lake (Turstini-watra in the twelfth century, and doubtless the property of a Thorstein at some earlier date); Thorpinsty, Cartmel and Torpenhow, Cumb. (Thorfinn's *teigr* and *haugr*); Uckmanby, perhaps from Ögmund); Ullswater (Ulf's); Ulverston (*Domesday*, Ulvrestune, and not Ulf's, but Ulfar's); Windermere (Hodgson Hinde's guess that this was Symeon's Wonwaldremere, A.D. 791, is quite unsupported; twelfth century Wynander-mare, the lake of Wynand, perhaps Vé-ánund). All these places seem to give the names of settlers, among which one or two might be claimed as rather Danish than Norse; but, on the other hand, the Irish names imply immigration from the west, or, at least, connexion with the Gallgael, while the bulk are such as might be found in Iceland.

In a book which has been used somewhat incautiously by historians (*The Northmen in Cumberland and Westmorland*, 1856), the late Robert Ferguson derived many Cumbrian place-names from names and nicknames taken at random from all sources: *e.g.* Butterlip-howe, at Grasmere, he made the howe of Buthar Lipr, Buthar the handyman; whereas "butter," which elsewhere in England means a bittern (butterbump), seems to be often used in Cumbria for "a road," Irish *bothar*, a loanword brought in by the Gallgael, and perhaps this odd name merely means the hill where there was a gate or a rise on the ancient track which passes the place.

Every Guide to the Lakes gives as "Norse testnames" *beck* and *bowse*, *fell* and *force*, *guard* and *gill* (the form "ghyll" is a modern monstrosity), *hause* and *holm* (though "holm" is not confined to Norse names), *lathe* and *lund*, *ness*, *raise* (a cairn) and *rake*, *scale* and *scree*, *tarn* and *thwaite*. A few notable places are: Arklid (hillside of the ergh or shieling); Armathwaite (Ermitethait, about 1230, the hermit's field); Askham (twelfth century Askhome, *i.e.* Ashholm); Axle (like Öxl, in Iceland, the shoulder); Barrow (the island of Barrow-in-Furness, Barray in sixteenth century, *Barr-ey*, where barley grew); Biglands and Biggar (Biggarth, where "bigg" grew); Blakeholme (*bleikr*, pale yellow); Blawith (*blá-viðr*, like Bláskógr, in Iceland, black-wood); Blowick on Ullswater (*blá-vik*); Brathay (*breið-á*, broad river);

Brisco (Byrescaye, *birk-skógr*); Butterilket, in Eskdale
(Brotherulkil, twelfth century, perhaps *brautar-hólls-
kelda*, the spring at the hill on the Roman road; or
-ölkelda, the "ale-spring," bubbling well); Catchede-
cam is a corruption of the dialectic "cat-stee-camb,"
the ridge of the cat's path, from *stigi*, like Stye-head;
Claif (*kleif*); Cleator (Cletergh, the shieling near
rocks); Corby (Chorkeby in 1120, from *korki*, Gaelic
for oats, a word used in the *Edda*); Dillicar (*dilkar*,
small sheep-folds); Feet for a low-lying meadow, the
Icelandic *fit*, is common; Gascow (thirteenth century,
Garthscoh, *garðs-skógr*); Gatescarth (*geits-skarð*);
Grain, a tributary brook, is used like *grein* in Iceland :
Greta (*grjótá*, stony-river); Grisedale (*grís-dalr*, where
swine were fed); Hammer often represents the Icelandic *hamarr*, a rock; Haverthwaite, Haverbreck
(*hafra-brekka*, goats'-bank, it is doubtful if *hafrar*
was used for "oats" at the period of settlement);
Hellbeck and Hellgill (*hella*, slate, or *hellir*, cave);
Ireby and Ireleth (the Irishmen's farm and hillside);
Kellet (Keldelith, fourteenth century, hillside of the
spring); Keswick, near Cardew, is in the Holme
Cultram Register Keldesik, the water-course (A.-S.
sic, Icelandic *sik*) of the well, which may explain
the name of the town on Derwentwater, though in
1292 it is written Keswyk, and may refer to the inlet
of the lake on which it stands. Near it, however, is
Lyzzick, the *hlíð-sik*, which seems analogous. This
name, like others, may have been brought from the
east of England by Danish settlers after the period of
the first immigration. The old inhabited site which

Keswick superseded was Crosthwaite. Leath Ward is the district on the *Híð* or slope of the hills of Edenside; so Lyth, in the Gilpin Valley, and Liddale, in 1292, was spelt Lythdale. Musgrave probably means the moss where peat was dug; Natland, Nateby and Naddale refer to *naut*, "neat," cattle; Orgrave (Ouregraue in *Domesday*) is a place where iron-ore was dug at early times; perhaps pre-Norse, but possibly *aur-gröf.* Raisbeck and Raisthwaite may be so called from the cairns (*hreysar*) near them, like Dunmail Raise. Rossett and Rosthwaite may refer, like Rusland, to the name of Hrólf, or to *hross*, a horse, like Hrossaholt in Iceland. Sawrey and Sowerby are "sour" lands, from *saurr*. Scafell is the mountain of precipices with chasms in them, perhaps *Skora-fell;* Scarthgap is the pass through a notch (*skarð*) in the hills. Southerfell is the Icelandic *Sauðafell,* like Fairfield (*Færfjall*), the hill where sheep pasture; Sunbrick (Swenebrec in the fourteenth century) is *svína-brekka*, the bank where swine feed. Swarthmoor (*svartr*) and Sweden (*sviðinn*) How are places where the copse or heather was burnt. Thrimby, in *Domesday*, is Tiernebi, *tjarnabær*, the farm of the tarns?; Tilberthwaite, in the twelfth century, Tildesburgthwait, the field of the tent-shaped hill (*tjaldberg*); and Torver, the ergh on the peat moss. Ulpha and Ullscarth recall the fact that wolves roamed the hills; Warcop and Warwick, Warthole (*hóll*, a hill) and Warton are named from their beacons (*varða*). Watendlath was Wattendland, *temp.* Richard I. Whale is perhaps simply *hváll*, the hill, used as a place-name in Iceland.

Wythop was formerly Withorppe and Wyth-thorp, the village in the wood; Harbyrn, the high borran, and Wythburn, the wide borran, or pile of stones, a word borrowed by the Vikings from Ireland and frequently used in the Lake District for natural rocky places and for ancient ruins, like Borrans Ring, the remains of the Roman camp at Ambleside. Wyth-burn, however, appears in a sixteenth century will as Wythbotten, and this word *botn,* usually Englished "bottom," is often found in Cumbria and Yorkshire for the head—not basin—of a valley, as in Iceland.

In the northern fringe of the Lake District there are also many names with Blen, Caer, Pen, etc., which show Cymric survivals, proving that the Welsh of Cumberland, as well as the Angles already settled there, lived side by side with the Norse immigrants. All the Norse place-names indicate the domestic life of a race occupied in farming: there is nothing heroic about them in the way of sites consecrated to the memory of battles—though battles were fought,—or of heathen rites—though heathen gods were still remembered, if not worshipped. One place in Westmorland, Hoff Lunn (*lundr*) may signify such practices, but it is the exception. The supposed references to Thor, Odin, and Baldr as gods commemorated in place-names are illusory; and yet the Gosforth Cross shows that about the year 1000 these myths were current, side by side, with Christianity. The survivals of Norse in the dialect point the same way. To berry (*berja,* thresh); the boose (*báss,* cow-shed); the brandrith (*brandreið,* tripod for baking); elding (as in Icelandic, fuel); the festingpenny (*festa*, to stipulate, compare "festermen") given to a servant on hiring; galt (*galti*, a pig); garn (*garn*, yarn); gowpen (*gaupn*, the two hands-full); hagworm (*höggormr*, viper); handsel (*handsöl*, bargain); keslop, rennet from a calf (*kæsir*, rennet, *hlaup*, curd); laik, to play (*leika*); lathe, a barn (*hlaða*); ley, a scythe (*lé*); leister, a salmon-spear (*ljóstr*); look, to weed (*lok*, weeds); meer, a boundary (*mæri*); rake and outrake, path up which sheep are driven (*reka*, to drive); reckling, the weakest of the litter (*reklingr*, an outcast); rean or raine, the unploughed strips between the riggs in the ancient system of cultivation (*rein*); rise, brushwood (*hrís*); sieves, rushes from which rush-lights were made (*sef*); sime, straw-rope (*síma*, rope); sile, a sieve for milk (*síli*); skemmel, a bench (*skemill*); skill, to shell peas (*skilja*); skut, the hind-end board of a cart (*skutr*, the stern); stang, the cart-shaft (*stöng*); stee, a ladder (*stigi*); stower, a stake (*staurr*); twinter and trinter, sheep of two and three winters old (*tvævetr* and *þrévetr*); quey, a young cow (*kviga*);—these are a few of the distinctive dialect words, not all confined to Cumberland, but all apparently surviving from the Norse farmers (taken from the glossary compiled by the Rev. T. Ellwood, English Dialect Society, 1895). Dr. Prevost, in his *Cumberland Glossary*, enumerates over a hundred different words "applied to beating and striking"; but these are chiefly common English and some are modern slang. The old dialect words from the Norse, as Mr. Ellwood points out, are chiefly and almostly entirely such as were used in domestic life and in farming. Two ancient Norse customs are preserved in the word "arvals," the food of a funeral feast, and "dordum" expressing the uproar of the door-doom (*dura-dómr*) or court of law held at the door of the offender's house; for a description of which, in curious circumstances, see *Eyrbyggja Saga* (chap. 55).

There is no central place named Thingwall in Cumberland, as there is in Wirral, in Lancashire, and in Dumfriesshire (Tinwald). Thiefstead, near Shap, in Westmorland, was formerly Thengheved, and may be the site of a Thingstead. On the Roman road through the heart of the Lake District, at a point where cross-ways are thought to have run north and south, is the curious terraced mound of Fell Foot, in Little Langdale, resembling the Tynwald Hill in the Isle of Man and the similar Thingmote formerly existing in Dublin. The custom of holding an assembly at a hill was perhaps copied by the Vikings from Ireland: see Prof. A. Bugge's *Caithreim Ceallachain Caisil*, p. 123, where an instance is given of the Irish practice. There are, however, no towns in this area, like the Five Boroughs—Carlisle being ruinous from Halfdan to William Rufus—in which we might have found traces of Scandinavian life, and documentary evidence fails us, except in the Gospatric charter, for Domesday Book touches only the southern border of the district. Roger of Wendover's mention of a king Jukil or Inkil of Westmorland (974) is in too corrupt a passage to trust; or a Norse king Jökull or perhaps Ingjalld might be imagined, for the identification of this king

(whom Symeon calls Nichil) with Idwal of Wales is
not convincing, and the fact that eight years previously
Westmorland was harried by Thord of York suggests
that the Viking colony had been growing too important.
The tradition of a king at the port of Ravenglass,
Aveling—perhaps a corruption of Abloic, the Welsh
equivalent of Olaf (whence Haveloc)—is too shadowy
to build upon. We can only say that the monuments and place-names of Cumberland point to
an early and powerful colony of Norse in touch with
Ireland and the Isles, and that towards the end of the
tenth century, as the Gosforth and other crosses show,
no other part of the Viking world could surpass this
district in literary and artistic culture. Situated on
the shore of the Irish Sea, which was a Viking lake,
and on the main road from the English east to the
Celtic west, the neighbourhood of Gosforth was
indeed geographically the focus of all the influences
which fostered the birth of the Edda poems. Wherever
they were composed, it was here that they were illustrated almost at the moment of their production. In
the Isle of Man—within view of the West Cumberland
shore—we find also Edda subjects in sculpture, but of
somewhat later date and in less fulness. Heysham,
Halton, and Penrith show some examples of the same
art, but the centre of this Edda-illustrating region and
the richest in remains is Gosforth with its crosses and
hogbacks, and the contemporary relics at the neighbouring sites of Waberthwaite, Muncaster, Beckermet
Haile, St. Bees, Workington, Brigham, Great Clifton,
Bridekirk, Dearham, Gilcrux, Isel, Cross-Canonby,

Aspatria, Plumbland, and Bromfield.   (See *Early Sculptured Crosses of the Diocese of Carlisle*, by Calverley and Collingwood.)

It was amongst the Norse settlers of the tenth and eleventh centuries in northern England that, according to Prof. Sophus Bugge, the " Helgakviða " was composed.   The group of poems resembling this, "the finest heroic poems in the whole range of Northern Song," are attributed by Vigfússon and York Powell (*Corpus Poet. Bor.*, Introd.) to some nameless but inspired singer on some shore of the Irish Sea or in the Hebrides.   It was certainly in the land of the Cumbri, whether north or south of Solway, that a literary movement almost as important as that which created the Edda took place ; the creation of not only the folk-tales of Havelock and Horn, but also of those Arthurian tales which contain so many motives of the Viking Age, and confuse the ancient Celtic mythology with waifs and strays from ninth and tenth century history and from the folklore of the Norse, placing Arthur's court at " merry Carlisle," then the ruined city of the Romans and Angles, the adventures of Merlin in the Wood of Caledon after the famous battle of Arthuret in Cumberland, Gawain at Tarn Wadling in Inglewood, Blaise in Northumberland, Lancelot at Bamborough, and Urien of Reged in the region of the Roman Wall. All this seems to be a secondary result of the impulse to thought and action given by this great but forgotten settlement of the Norse in Cumberland and the districts round about it.

4. DUMFRIESSHIRE AND GALLOWAY.

A sister colony can be traced on the north shore of
the Solway, occupying the district between the Esk
and the Dee, with centre at Tinwald (Thingvellir)
near Dumfries, but extending into Kirkcudbrightshire
on the one hand, into Peeblesshire on the other, and
reaching inland as far as the main watershed between
east and west ; Liddesdale, Liddel's-dale, was the
Hlíð-dalr of the settlers, but the outlying parts of this
area no doubt owe their names in -beck, -gill, -rig, -fell,
-by and -thwaite to secondary settlement later than
the tenth century. It has been thought that the
original colony was planted in 876 by Halfdan, which
is possible ; but as the whole was afterwards within
the kingdom of the Strathclyde Cymru, and open to
the same influences as Cumberland, no sharp distinction can be drawn between the two districts; Danish
origins must have been overlaid by subsequent Norse
immigration. We find Cumberland names repeated
in Brydekirk, Lowther-hill and -ton, Newbigging,
Croglin, Dalton, Rockcliffe, Eskdale, Eaglesfield,
Whinfell, Aiket, Canonbie, etc. ; and similar forms in
Criffell, Arkland (compare Arklid), Kelton, Stanhope,
Rutnwell (*Rauð-vellir*), Lockerbie, Smallholm (*smali*,
small cattle, sheep and goats, compare Smallthwaite),
Tundergarth, Middlebie, Middleton, Burnswark
(*borrans-virki*, from the Gaelic loan-word *boireand*),
Closeburn (*Kil-Osbjörn*), Langholm, Broomholm, etc.

Gaelic and Welsh names, not infrequent in Cumberland, are more frequent north of Solway, and show that the settlement did not drive out the earlier population : there is no area so exclusively Scandinavian as to suggest that a clearance was made by forcible invasion ; but the Norse names are, as usual, thicker on the coast, and fade away thence inland. The name of the Solway itself can hardly be from that of the Selgovae who inhabited Galloway in Roman times ; the termination is surely the Norse *vágr*, a creek, and the characteristic of this estuary is its tidal bore ; whence one is tempted to connect it with *soll*, "swill," and *solmr*, "the swell of the sea."

The stone carvings of Dumfriesshire, so far as they can be judged from Mr. Romilly Allen's great volume on the Early Christian Monuments of Scotland, seem to be wholly of pre-Viking period. There are splendid works of the Anglian church at Ruthwell, Hoddam, Thornhill, Closeburn and elsewhere. The absence of relics of the Viking Age may perhaps be explained by their presence in the neighbourhood of Whithorn. We find, for example, an interesting series at Whithorn itself showing an evident transition from Anglian work to debased floral scrolls, hammerhead crosses, broken ring-plaits and ruder cutting, characteristic of the Viking period in Cumberland and Yorkshire. At Aspatria in Cumberland is a curious incised slab with the Norse *Swastika* ; this is paralleled by a slab from Craignarget on Luce Bay, and the hammerhead slab with rude crucifix and barbarous scroll-work from Kirkcolm on Loch Ryan resembles the

Addingham (Cumberland) cross and others, made for
Viking patrons in imitation of earlier models. Now,
as Iona was the burial-place of Hebridean chieftains,
so Whithorn must have been the mausoleum of the
notables of this coast ; and perhaps all who could
afford a monument, buried their dead at the famous
sanctuary of St. Ninian. This may explain the absence
of distinctively Viking-age work in Dumfriesshire,
though in Kirkcudbright there are many stones of
the tenth century which may have been carved for
the settlers without introducing any very characteristic
Viking ornament.

In Wigtownshire itself was another Norse colony,
no doubt connected with that in Dumfriesshire, and
yet divided by the hilly district west of the Dee,
in which there is a smaller proportion of Norse place-
names except on the coast-line. Here again Cumbrian
names are reduplicated, as Wigtown, Sorbie (Sowerby),
Broughton, Carleton, Glasserton, Ramsey, Tongue,
Gretna ; while Physgill (Fishcegil, *fiski-gil*), Eggerness
(ness of the Solway tidal-bore) and Fleet (*Fljót*) are
of similar form. In Njál's saga Beruvík, somewhere
near Whithorn, is named ; it has been found at
Burrow Head or Yarrock Bay, but there is also a
Berwick near Kirkcudbright. The farmers' loan-word
ergh is found again in another Arkland, and is common
as *-aroch*, while the Gaelic form appears in Airyland.

The origin of the settlement in Galloway, connected as it must be with the Gallgael (Galweithia
being the Latin from Galwyddel the Cymric equivalent of the Gaelic Gallgaidhel) is perhaps earlier,

though not much earlier, than that of the Cumberland
colony.   The Gallgael are first found in 854 or 855
in co. Tyrone, and next year as settled in northern
Ireland (Leathchuinn).   The Four Masters mention
Gofraith mac Feargus as invited by Kenneth mac
Alpin to strengthen Dalriada (south-west Scotland)
in 835, and he died as king of Insigall (the Hebrides)
in 852, the year in which Olaf the White came to
Ireland.   The name of Gofraith suggests that he was
-himself an early example of the mixed race, and by
835 the Norse were certainly attacking the Islands,
while in 839 the Ulster Annals and the Chronicle of
Huntingdon record invasion of Pictish territory.   Then
we find Olaf the White fighting Caittil Finn, or Ketil
Flatnef, with his Gallgael in Munster, 857, and subsequently in alliance with him, having married Ketil's
daughter Aud, after already marrying the daughter of
Kenneth.   It may have been a case of polygamy,
to which ninth-century Vikings were accustomed ;
but from what we know of Aud this is doubtful.
Now *Heimskringla* represents Ketil as Harald Fairhair's viceroy ; *Laxdæla* makes him his enemy.
Possibly Ketil at first left Norway to escape Harald,
and later was used as a stick to beat Olaf the White :
failing which, at a subsequent date, Harald Fairhair
came in person.   In any case Ketil and his party
were by no means subdued, and though the Irish
annals represent the Gallgael as renegades worse than
heathen, Aud, Helgi Magri and other connexions of
Ketil appear as Christians, or semi-Christianised.   It
is of Helgi, the Christian son-in-law of Ketil, that it is

said he worshipped Thor when he was at sea, or in danger, though praying to Christ when on shore.

From Ireland the Gallgael seem to have migrated about 860–870 to the islands and coasts of south-west Scotland, during the time when Olaf the White was extending his power in that direction. He wasted Pictland (Galloway?) in 866, and took Alclyde (Dumbarton) the capital of the Cymric realm in 870. In 875 Oistin, his son, is said to have been treacherously slain by the people of Alban ; and the identification of this Oistin (Eystein) with Thorstein the Red, another son of Olaf, whose conquests in northern Scotland must have been of a later date, has led to much confusion in the history of the period. In 877 a body of Danes, driven from Ireland by the Norse, crossed Scotland to Fife and fought Constantine at Dollar ; but no settlement is recorded as made. Meanwhile in 875 Halfdan had invaded Galloway, and the coast probably was open to other parties of Vikings. That the Northmen in these parts were not hostile to English Christians, is shown by the sojourn of St. Cuthbert's relics at Whithorn about this time. But that they soon became populous in the islands as far south as Man is shown by Harald's invasion, which cannot be later than about 880, and if it had occurred earlier it would have left some traces in the story of Eardwulf's pilgrimage. He and his companions, it will be remembered, are said to have left Whithorn on hearing of Halfdan's death, slowly returning along the coast. They could not have been in Galloway in such a time of tumult and

P

distress. The first definite settlement of Galloway, therefore, may be put at this date, simultaneously with that of Cumberland and Dumfriesshire. Thenceforward Galloway is to the Island kingdom as Caithness is to the Orkney earldom, a mainland colony of allies rather than dependents; and its subsequent history is bound up with that of Man and the Isles.

5. MAN AND THE ISLES.

We have seen that about 880 Man was already a Scandinavian colony. In the year 900 Vikings from Ireland, under the O'Ivars, ruling in Dublin and Limerick, invaded Scotland and killed King Domhnall at Dunottar; and three years later Ivar O'Ivar plundered Dunkeld, but was slain in Stratherne. This seems to suggest the extension of Irish Viking enterprise, after the invasion of Harald Fairhair, into and beyond the districts he had depopulated. In 914 Bard Ottarson, whose son Colla was lord of Limerick in 924, was killed in a sea fight off the Isle of Man by Ragnvald, afterwards king of York. At Brunanburh Bard's son Hárek was present, and Geleachan (one of the Irish names in *giolla*, adopted by the Gallgael), king of the Islands, was killed. In 940 the Insigall were plundered by King Muirceartach mac Neill, who himself had been taken prisoner by the Vikings three years earlier, but ransomed. In the middle of the century Morann, son of Connra the "fleet-king of Lewis," son of the king of Norway (or the Norse), is named in connexion with Limerick (Prof. A. Bugge,

Vikingerne, i., p. 178) together with Aedh, son of Echu, another Hebridean king, and Eirík, king of the Islands, whom Prof. Bugge identifies with Eirík Blóðöx, lately expelled from York and shortly to be killed at Stainmoor ; which fixes the date at about 953. We seem to see the Islands under Gallgael rulers, some of whom had relations with Limerick ; but no settled dynasty was in occupation.

To this period may perhaps be assigned the story told in *Landnáma* and the older version of *Droplaugarsona saga*, of a jarl Asbjörn Skerjablesi (Skerry-blaze) "who ruled in the Hebrides after Tryggvi (a form of Sigtrygg) and before Guthorm." He was attacked by the vikings Hólmfast Vethorm's son and his kinsman Grím, descended from Ketil Raum (of Romsdal), who slew him and carried his wife and daughter into captivity. If the dating of the story may be attempted, the event must have happened about 940, though the absence of detail makes it impossible to guess whereabouts was the jarldom of these three rulers.

In 961 the fleet of Olaf Cuaran's son and the Lagmenn of the Islands (Isle of Man ?) plundered Cork and carried their prey to Britain and to Mon-Conain (Anglesey) ; and these Lagmenn reappear with Magnus (Maccus), son of Harald, in 974, as attacking the south of Ireland. The English chronicles relate that Magnus Haraldsson was one of the kings who yielded submission to Eadgar, and he was probably son of Harald Sigtryggsson O'Ivar, lord of Limerick, who was killed in Connaught in 940 ; suggesting a

continued connexion of the Isle of Man with Limerick.
The name Magnus originates in Charlemagne; we
find also a Carlus, son of Olaf the White, killed in
battle 867, and his sword was one of the treasures of
Dublin carried off by King Maelseachlann in 995:
a Carlus mac Con was slain by Northmen in 960; his
name curiously recalls the mysterious Karl Hundason
of the next century, certainly not intended (as Skene
thought) for a term of reproach (see Rhys' *Celtic
Britain*, p. 267). A Magnus Bjarnarson of Limerick
died in 968, and the name must have come into use
in hero-worship of the great enemy of the Vikings.

With Magnus Haraldsson we find the first fairly
ascertained dynasty of Man and the Isles: he died
about 977, and was succeeded by his brother Godred
(Godfrid), who fought a battle in Man (987) with Danes
from Dublin, who had been plundering in Dalriada,
and at Christmas had slain the abbot of Iona and
fifteen of his monks. This is about the time, though
the circumstances are not those, of the story told in
Njal's saga of Kári Sölmundarson and Njál's sons
Grím and Helgi, who landed in Man and forced
Godred to pay the tribute claimed by the king of
Norway. At a later date they attacked him again,
and slew Dungall his son, and then betook them to
Colonsay, where they stayed with jarl Gilli, who accompanied them to Orkney and married a daughter
of jarl Sigurd. Godred's kingdom evidently did not
extend over the whole of the Islands; he died in
989, succeeded by his sons Ragnvald and Kenneth,
and his grandson Svein (Suibhne), son of Kenneth.

About this time Olaf Tryggvason before his conversion buccaneered on the coasts of Wales, Man and the
Hebrides : and Svein, afterwards king of Denmark
and England, also attacked the island from his head-
quarters in Wales.

At the battle of Clontarf (1014), beside the men of
Orkney and Caithness are mentioned, in *The Wars of
the Gaedhil and the Gaill*, the hosts of Mān, Skye,
Lewis, Kintyre, Argyll, "Cillemuine" (St. Davids)
and the people dwelling in the British land of "Cornbliteoc" or "Cor na liagog," which Skene thought
might mean Galloway : can "Cornbliteoc" be a
mistranscription of some such word as "Combraeog"?
After this battle, which broke up the Norse power of
Orkney, jarl Gilli—who did not go to Clontarf—continued to rule Colonsay and the surrounding islands,
but the Scottish chief Finlaec held Moray and Ross
independently of either Scotland or Orkney, and
perhaps annexed the northern Hebrides. Argyll, the
Dalir of the Norse, was held by a jarl Melkolf
(Malcolm), who also held Galloway, for we find
Kári Sölmundarson staying with him, apparently at
Whithorn, soon after the battle. Man continued
under the same family ; Svein (Suibhne), the last king
of the old Gallgael line, died in 1034, after which
Thorfinn, the great jarl of Orkney, extended his
dominion over all Scotland except Strathclyde, Fife
and Lothian, often making Galloway his head-quarters.
His dominion over the Isles probably meant little
more than that he took tribute and was recognised
as over-lord. In 1031 King Knút received the

submission of Malcolm of Scotland, together with two
kings, named Maelbaethe and Jehmarc, in whom
Skene (*Celtic Scotland*, i., p. 397) saw Macbeth, son of
Finlaec, independent ruler of Moray, and Imergi the
king of Argyll or Dalir, whose great-great-grandson
was Sumarlidi (d. 1166). We have therefore reason
to think that the kingdom of Man and the Isles did
not then include the northern Hebrides ; the central
part of the group, at least, must have been under the
- Gallgael (not purely Celtic) rulers of Argyll.

The surnames and place-names of Man have been
studied by Mr. A. W. Moore, and the early monuments by Mr. P. M. C. Kermode, in books which
illustrate the Scandinavian settlement, its great importance and its limits, with a copiousness which
makes it needless to give any detail in a general sketch
of a wide subject such as this is. Prof. Alex. Bugge
has also written an interesting chapter, chiefly on the
Scandinavian crosses, in his *Vikingerne*. There are
some peculiarities in the place-names, noted by Mr.
Moore, which distinguish Man from Cumberland :
-*by* is common, and he rightly adds that it is both
Danish and Norwegian ; *thorpe* is found once, *toft*
twice ; *thwaite*, *beck*, *with*, *tarn* and *force* are absent,
but *haugh*, *dale*, *fell*, *garth* and *gill* are frequent ; and
he concludes that the settlers in Man were less Danish
than those of East Anglia and Eastern Ireland, and
more so than those of Cumbria and the Hebrides.
This was no doubt the case ; but the reasons for the
absence of some " test-words " may be simply the
absence of need for them. Gaelic names of streams

and waterfalls being ready made, *beck* and *force* were not needed ; lakes being unknown, there are no *tarns ;* villages unfamiliar, as in Cumbria, *thorpe* was little used ; the *thwaite* in its proper sense being infrequent, and *mǒr*, the timber-wood, devastated, leaving only *skógar* of copse, these words were not applied, though existent in the language of the settlers. For the rest there are many similarities between Manx nomenclature and Cumbrian : compare Peel with Peel Castle in Furness, etc., Surby with Sowerby, Kirby with Kirkby, Scarsdale with Scarthgap, Cammall with Camfell ; and Fleswick, Colby, Ramsey, Raby, Sulby (Soulby), Kneebe (Knipe), Kirkbride, etc., are identical. Several Manx words are seen in the names both of Man and Cumbria : *korki* (oats), *cnoc* (knock, knoll), *parak* (parrock, " park," also transplanted to Iceland), *dob* (dub, pool), *spooyt* (waterfall, as in Gill Spout), *bayr* (Gaelic *bothar*, Cumbrian " butter " and " bare "), *glas* (stream, as in Ravenglass), *borrane* (Gaelic *boireand*, Cumbrian " borran, burn ")—these are loan-words which suggest the borrowing of language from Man by the settlers in Cumbria as well as by those on the north of Solway ; and the language was the mixed speech of the Gallgael.

Turning to the monuments we have resemblances even more striking. We have seen that in Cumbria and in its neighbourhood there is a series of crosses dating from the end of the tenth to some time in the eleventh century, with carvings illustrating the Edda. At Halton we have Sigurd the Völsung ; and the same subject is found at Andreas, Jurby and Malew in Man.

At Heysham we have the gods at Ragnarök ; Mr.
Kermode finds at Andreas Odin fighting the Fenris-
wolf. At Gosforth we have Heimdal with his horn,
repeated at Jurby. Even if all the identifications of
Prof. A. Bugge and Mr. Kermode are not accepted,
there are still enough to show that Edda subjects were
illustrated in both districts on crosses put up as monuments of Christian burial. Of Runic inscriptions
there is a wealth in these Manx stones, and from the
language and lettering it is concluded that the inscribed crosses date from 1040 onwards ; and further,
that there was some relation to East Gothia (Sweden)
and Jæderen (Norway) in the carvers of these runes.
One stone (Michael, No. 104) is thought by Prof.
Sophus Bugge to be Swedish in character, though on
the whole the language is Norse, and of the eleventh
and twelfth centuries. But while the inscribed stones,
which are not paralleled by Cumbrian crosses, are comparatively late, there are also some uninscribed which
may be of the tenth century. One of these is the
cross which bears the figure of a bishop, and is
connected by Mr. Kermode with bishop Roolwer
(Hrólfr), mentioned in 1060 ; a cross which, however,
has a close resemblance to Cumbrian stones showing
the debased spiral forms imitated from Anglian floral
scrolls, though at the same time it shows Celtic
motives absent in Cumbria, with no special Scandinavian character. Its Madonna can be matched by
Yorkshire stones earlier than the eleventh century.
The conclusion seems to be that perhaps a hundred
years earlier than Roolwer there was a Christian

church on the island under Godred or his predecessor Magnus—as indeed is not impossible : for a realm
in touch with England on the one hand, and Ireland
on the other, inhabited by a settled population as
Man then was, must have assimilated itself to its sur-
roundings. The modern name of the bishopric still
recalls the old kingdom which was coextensive with it,
Sodoriensis et Manniæ, of the Sudreyjar (South-isles,
Hebrides) and Man; abbreviated into "Sodor. and
Man." It need hardly be said that such a form as
"Sodor" or "the Sodors" is a barbarism when used
for Sudreyjar.

Thorfinn, the great jarl of Orkney, whose power and
presence in Galloway overshadowed Manx independence, died in 1064, about which time we find Godred
Sigtryggsson on the throne. He sent aid to the Norse
invasion of England in 1066, and some of the few
who escaped from Stamford Bridge took refuge with
him. Among these was Godred Crovan, son of
Harold the Black of Islay (as Munch showed, not
"of Iceland"), who eventually wrested Man from
Fingall, Godred Sigtryggsson's heir, about 1075. He
set over the northern islands his son Lagman, who
succeeded him on the Manx throne as a monarch of
an independent power. To reassert the ancient rights
of Norway over the Islands, Magnus Barefoot invaded
at the end of the eleventh century, and placed Ingimund over the northern Hebrides, and Ottar over Man.
Both fell in revolts, and Magnus Barefoot invaded
again, leaving the islands desolated, though not without
some attempt to restore the prosperity of the Manx.

Then followed a period of anarchy until 1113, when Olaf Bitling, son of Godred Crovan, was elected king of Man. His youth had been spent at the court of Henry I. of England; he married the daughter of Fergus, lord of Galloway, a granddaughter of Henry I., and reigned in peace for forty years, strengthening his kingdom by alliances. His daughter married Sumarlidi (Somerled), the Gallgael lord of Dalir (Argyll), ancestor of the Macdonalds of the Isles, and partisan of the romantic adventurer Malcolm mac Eth, who had been a monk of Furness Abbey under the name of Wymund (Vémund) and threw Scotland into confusion by his claims and attempts. After Olaf Bitling's death his son and successor, Godred, came into collision with Sumarlidi, and by the naval battle of 1156 was forced to surrender part of his kingdom of the Isles. Two years later Sumarlidi invaded Man; Godred fled to Norway, but returned after a six years' absence to hold his throne until 1187, when he was succeeded by his son Ragnvald.

The division of the Isles left Man in possession of the northern Hebrides, whereas those from Ardnamurchan Point southward remained in the hands of the Argyll family, first under Dubhgall and then under Ragnvald, Sumarlidi's sons. Consequently in 1187, King Ragnvald of Man held Man and the northern isles, while King Ragnvald of Argyll held the central part of the whole group. Galloway in 1160 ceased to be independent; Malcolm of Scotland reduced it to the condition of a province, as he also reduced Moray, where he expelled the Viking or Gallgael inhabitants and replaced them by " his own people." This extension of the Scottish power at the expense of the Norse went on during the reigns of William the Lion (1166-1214) and Alexander II. (1214-1249), who crushed repeated revolts in Galloway, Moray and Ross, and added all the mainland, including Caithness, to the Scottish kingdom. The last act of Alexander II. was an unsuccessful attempt to add the Hebrides to his power.

Ragnvald of Man reigned for thirty-eight years. One of the incidents of his troubled reign was an attack on the island by King John of England (1210), invading a country until then no part of the English realm, but politically under Norway. On Ragnvald's deposition by his brother Olaf the Black, Hákon Hákonarson, king of Norway, tried to reassert his power over the Hebrides, which had ceased to pay the accustomed tribute ; but the expedition he sent under Hákon Ospak was defeated by Olaf the Black, who remained in Man until 1237, with Godred Don, his nephew, as viceroy over the northern Isles ; the central Hebrides being still under the family of Sumarlidi, whose great-grandson John, lord of the Isles, was in possession at the time when Olaf the Black's sons, Harald and Ragnvald (Ronald), having died, there was a failure in the direct descent of the Manx crown (1249), which gave Alexander II. his opportunity to annex the Islands—an opportunity which failed on this occasion, but recurred before long to his successor.

Alexander II. had tried at first to win the Hebrides by negotiations with Hákon of Norway, on the ground

that the Islands had been wrested from the Scottish
kingdom by Magnus Barefoot, but the Norwegian
crown maintained a claim which had held good for
some four centuries.   At last, however, it was not so
much a question of ancient rights as of practical politics.
The kingdom of Scotland, once a small realm on the
east coast (p. 131), had grown into a great power,
which could hardly tolerate upon its border an alien
state, turbulent and dangerous in the semi-independ-
-ence of petty rulers.   Consequently Alexander III.,
on coming of age (1262), prepared to carry out his
father's policy of annexing the Islands.   Hákon of
Norway next year bought a great fleet to resist the
threatened encroachment.   He was joined by Magnus,
king of Man, the last son of Olaf the Black, and
Dugall, lord of the Isles.   After their triumphant
progress to the Clyde, Alexander was ready to make
terms, claiming only Arran, Bute and the Cumbraes.
A storm wrecked the Norse fleet, and an accidental
encounter brought on the battle of Largs.   Both sides
claimed the victory, but the effect of the battle was to
send Hákon north to Orkney, where he died soon
afterwards, and Magnus of Man did homage to the
Scottish Crown.   In 1266 a treaty between Norway
and Scotland ceded Man and the Hebrides to Alexander ; the ecclesiastical rights of the archbishop of
Trondhjem being retained.   King Eirík of Norway
married the Princess Margaret of Scotland, and it was
only by the death of their daughter Margaret in
Orkney (1290) that the last link was broken.
. But still the Islands kept many of their Norse

characteristics. We have seen that they were the
home of the Gallgael, never purely Scandinavian.
From the first some of the Norse who settled there
took Gaelic surnames, adopted Celtic Christianity,
imitated Irish poetry and art, intermarried with natives.
The name a person bore was no complete test of his
race, and the ultimate prevalence of Gaelic as the
spoken language, brought about by the political union
with Scotland, has little relation to the ethnography
of the Hebrides and Highlands. Prof. A. Bugge has
discussed (in his notes to Duald MacFirbis on the
Fomorians and the Norsemen) the pedigree of the
Macleods, of which a variant is given in Skene's *Celtic
Scotland;* and supposes that the two divisions of
the clan, Siol Tarquil and Siol Tormod, or family
of Thorkell and Thormôd—two chieftains of Skye
about 1230—were descended from Ljót (Leod) of
the twelfth century, mentioned in *Orkneyinga-saga,*
although the usual tradition deduces them from Ljót,
son of Olaf the Black (died 1237). In any case the
pedigree comes from the Norse. The macLeans and
the Morrisons, hereditary sheriffs of Lewis, deduce
from Gillemuire, whose Gaelic name disguises the
fact that he was son of Helga the Fair, daughter of
Harald, son of "Old Ivar, king of Lochlann." The
macCorquhadales of Argyll derive from Thorketill.
The macDonalds of the Isles are from Sumarlidi and
his Norse wife; Clan Alastair is from the same source.
The Nicolsons of Skye come from Olaf, son of
"Turcinn" of Dublin. The names of macDougal
(Dubhgall, "Dane"), Lamont (Lagman), macLachlan

(Lochlan), show their Scandinavian origin. MacAskill (Asketil), MacIver, MacRimmon (Hromund), Mac Aulay of Lewis (from Olaf—the MacAulays of Argyll are from Amalgaidh), Clan Ranald (Ragnvald) are all Scandinavian in name, though from the beginning, no doubt, not of unmixed Scandinavian blood. The clans of the mainland, by their pedigrees, are of Celtic origin.

In Gaelic, most of the shipping terms are Norse, according to Dr. Macbain; and most of the place-names of the coast are obviously Scandinavian, though often Gaelicised and not easy to recognise on a modern map. In a paper read to the Viking Club (*Saga-book*, ii., pp. 50 *seq.*), Miss A. Goodrich Freer gives a list of Gaelic words of non-Celtic origin, as collected by the late Father Allan Macdonald in the Outer Hebrides, from which the following are examples with the Icelandic equivalents:—aoinidh (enni), brow of hill; crò (kró), pen-fold; cuisle (kvísl), branch of stream; faothail (vadill in Shetland, vaðð), ford; haf (haf), ocean; hawn (hafn), haven; luithean (ljóri), louvre, smoke-vent; mealbhach (mel-bakki), links; mol (möl), gravel; nàbuidh (ná-búi), neighbour; òb (hóp), tidal bay; oda (oddi), tongue of land; rustal (ristill), plough; saoithean (seiðr, with diminutive), saithe; scàireag (skári with diminutive), young gull; sgeir (sker), skerry; sparran (sperra), rafter; trosg (thorsk), cod. In Outer Hebridean place-names very many terminations are Norse, more or less corrupted: -val (fell), -breck, -berg, -haug, for a hill; -ay, for island; -lam, -um (hólmr), for an islet;

-ort, -ford, -art (fjord) ; -vag, -way, -vik, for bay ; -ey
(eiǒ), for isthmus ; -geo (gjá), for a cleft; -oss.(óss),
for a river's mouth ; -brok (borg), for a fort ; -vallar,
-wall (vellir), field ; -bost (bústaǒr), -bol, -pool, (ból),
-stul (perhaps stóll, a seat), -ary (ergh, as used
also in Cumberland, Lancashire and Yorkshire, a
dairy-farm), for various kinds of farmsteads ; -vat
(vatn), for lake ; -a, -ai (á), for a river ; strom (straumr),
for a sea-current ; -skeir (sker), reef of rocks ; -nish,
-ness and -mul (múli), for a point of land ; -gil, becoming in Uist -gir, for a dell.   Adjectives used in place-
names are breidha and smuk (*smuga* is in Icelandic a
narrow hole, in Cumberland "smoot" is the sheep's
door in a fence-wall), for broad and narrow ; hà and
lai (hár and lágr), for high and low. Names of animals
in compounds are gaas (gás), so (sauǒr, sheep), lam,
calv, arne (örn, eagle), hest and ros.   Sigurd, Björn,
Grím and Eirík appear in the names of places in
these outer islands.

In a paper for the Viking Club by Mr. R. L.
Bremner (*Saga-book*, iii., p. 373) many details of
Norse place-names in the Southern Hebrides and
Argyll are given, with the help of Professor Mackinnon.
"In the Lewis it has been calculated the place-names
are about four Norse to one Gaelic ; in Skye as three
to two ; in Barvas (N.W. of Lewis) as twenty-seven to
one ; in Uig as thirty-five to four.   In Islay there is
one Norse to two Gaelic, in Kintyre one to four ; in
Arran and the Isle of Man one to eight. Jura has a
very few." Professor Mackinnon derives Jura from
Dyr-ey, "deer island," and *dýr* reappears in Ben

Diurinis (dýranes) on Loch Etive, Duirinish in Skye, and Durness in Sutherland. Lussa (Laxá), Asdale (ask-dalr), Sannaig (Sandvík), Bladda, like Pladda on the Clyde and Fladda near Mull (Flatey), are other names originally Norse in Jura. In Islay Loch Gruinart is the "green fjord"; compare Snizort in Skye, Enard, Knoydart, Moydart; in Melfort and Broadford a fuller form is preserved, still more in Seaforth. The word *bústaðr* (homestead) which in the outer isles becomes -bost or -bust, is shortened in Islay into -bus, as Cragabus, Kinnabus, Lyrabus, Coulabus; or from the form *bólstaðr* is Nereabols (in 1588 written Nerra-bollsadh); Robolls and Grobolls. Trudernish, like Trotternish in Skye, and Trodday may be from *tröð* (gen. *traðar*), a pasture or cattle-pen, the -nish for *nes*, having its sibilant softened after the "slender" vowel according to Gaelic usage. In Mull, Ar-os means "river's mouth"; Glenforsay and Assapol have Norse elements.

In Argyll, among the islands are Canna (possibly the canons' isle, as this was Church property—see an article by W. G. Collingwood in the *Antiquary*, 1906), Gometra, Ulva, Staffa (from the basalt pillars), Oronsay (not St. Oran's, but Orfiris-ey, the "island at ebb-tide"), Gigha (in Hákon's saga Gud-ey), Shuna, Eriska (Eric's), Kerrera (Kjarbarey), Lunga, Torsay and Scarba. Ashore are Knapdale, Ormsary, Skip-ness (in 1262 Schyph-inche, but not an island). In Kintyre are Sunadale, Torrisdale, Saddell, Rhonadale, Ifferdale, Ugadale—most from personal names; Lussa (Laxá), Smerby, Askomill, Stafnish, Sanda, etc.

In Bute, the oldest form of Rothesay is Rothersay, perhaps Hrothgar's ey or á. Ascog is like Ayscough, in Lancashire,—the ash-wood *ask-skógr*. Arran has a few Norse names; Brodick (anciently Brathwik, broad-bay), Goat-fell, Scordale, Glaister (-stadr), Ormidale, Glen Sherraig (in 1590 Sherwik). And in the Clyde, Kumreyjar (Cumbraes) was the Norse name for the isles of the Cumbri or Strathclyde Welsh.

One of the most interesting names is Pabay, variously spelt, for there are many examples in the Hebrides as well as in the Orkneys and Shetland. We know from the Saga form, Papey, that it means the island of the priests, *Papar ;* and we know from Dicuil that the Irish hermits were driven from their "deserts" by the Norse early in the ninth century, also from *Landnáma* that the same thing happened later in Iceland. The Rev. E. McClure (*Saga-book of the Viking Club*, i., p. 269) has suggested that the word, like *Kirkja*, was learnt by the early Vikings from the Goths of the Roman Empire, Christianised from Greek influences, whence also the German *pfaffe*. There is no doubt that the externals, and some of the teaching, of Christianity were known to the pagan Scandinavians long before they became converts ; the earliest descriptions of their temples in Iceland tell us that the apse was a feature of the building, and much of their mythology was a distorted glimpse of Christian beliefs. The name must have been given to these islands of the Papar at the time when the priests were first driven away, not in

Q

subsequent generations when the Irish or English word for "priest" was learnt.

When they became Christianised they set up grave-monuments here or elsewhere. At Kilbar in Barra is a cross with Scandinavian runes; another from St. Mannock's in Bute has, in runes, "Krus thine (let?) Guthle(if)," raised to the memory of one unknown. But as Galloway settlers were perhaps taken to Whithorn for burial, so the chiefs of the Isles were buried at Iona. Most of the monuments preserved there are either much earlier or much later than the period when distinctively Scandinavian ornament was given to these carvings, but there is one stone (figured by W. G. Collingwood in the *Saga-book of the Viking Club*, iii., p. 305) formerly in the chapel of St. Oran but now kept in the Cathedral, which is different from all the rest. On one side it bears the usual Scandinavian dragon with irregular interlacing; on the other a ship with its crew and a smith with his hammer, anvil and pincers. The resemblance of this to Manx crosses suggests that it may have been the tombstone of a king of Man.

Minor antiquities of the Viking Age are not in-frequent in the Hebrides and neighbouring parts of Scotland. The Hunterston brooch found near Largs with runic inscriptions perhaps of the tenth century, and other penannular brooches, are described in Dr. Anderson's *Scotland in Early Christian Times* (ii. 1). Pairs of "tortoise" brooches have been found in Islay and Tiree, and examples in Barra and Sanday; weapons in interments at Islay, Mull, Barra, Sanday and St. Kilda. A howe known as the Carnan-a-Bhairraich, in Oronsay, was explored in 1891, and found to contain brooches, beads, a ring, a knife and a net-sinker, beside boat-rivets; it seems as though the "man from Barra" was buried in his boat with his wife—possibly a case of "suttee," which was not unknown. At Kiloran Bay in Colonsay, Mr. MacNeill, in 1882, found a ship-burial with sword, axe, shield-boss, cauldron, etc., and a pair of scales and stycas of the archbishop of York, 831–854; also a horse's skeleton of which the hind leg had been cut before interment (*Saga-book of Viking Club*, v., p. 172).

It was not more than a generation later that Örlyg, who had been brought up in the Hebrides by bishop Patrick, set forth to Iceland "with wood for building a church, and a plenarium and an iron bell, a golden penny and consecrated earth to be put under the corner pillars. The bishop told him to land where two mountains rose out of the sea, . . . and there build a church and consecrate it to St. Columba" (*Landnáma*, i. 12). From this it is evident that even in the ninth century the Vikings in the Hebrides were already beginning to be Christianised, though imperfectly: for at Esjuberg, in Iceland, Örlyg and his family, when the church was built, seem to have worshipped, not Christ, but Columba.

6. The Earldom of Orkney.

That the earliest Norse settlers in Orkney and
Shetland found Irish priests in the islands, is known
from the names of Papa Stour, Papa Little and Papa
in Scalloway, Papal in Unst and Yell, and Papil in
Burra (Shetland), also Papa in Westray and Stronsay,
Paplay in South Ronaldsay and in Holm, and Papdale
near Kirkwall (Orkney). It has been remarked (p. 241)
that the word *Papar* for "priests" must have been
brought by the Norse; it shows that, contrary to
Dasent's opinion, the Shetlands were not uninhabited,
and that the heathen invaders recognised the priests
from the first. The persistence of the names Rinansey
(St. Ninian's Isle), Enhallow (Holy Isle), and Damsey
(St. Adamnan's Isle) in Orkney, and St. Ninian's Isle in
Shetland, together with the preservation of chapels of
early Celtic type, suggests that the priests were not
exterminated, in spite of a local tradition in Unst
(quoted by the Rev. A Sandison, *Saga-book of the
Viking Club*, i. 244) that the Picts fought until only
a priest and his son were left, and they perished
refusing to tell the secret of the heather-ale, as in the
Highland story picturesquely retold by Niel Munro
in *The Lost Pibroch*. Early dedications to Ninian,
Columba, Brigit and Triduana may have survived the
invasion; and it is possible that some of the sculptured
stones with ogams may be pre-Norse. On the other
hand, in the ogams of the Bressay stone (Shetland)

some scholars read the name Naddodd, which is Norse; the ornament, with ring-plaits and a peculiar form of interrupted double-strand interlacing, cannot be earlier than the tenth century; and the "son of the Druid" named on it, if that is a true reading, has a parallel at Rushen, Isle of Man, as the priest, horsemen and beasts reappear at Maughold (No. 67, Kermode's *Manx Crosses*). Again, the head between monsters on the Papil stone (Shetland) is seen also at Braddan (No. 69, *Manx Crosses*). The twelfth-century Maeshowe runes and "Thurbiarn" runes at Cunningsburgh have points of resemblance to Manx runes. There is an evident link between Man and the northern islands which is not without importance in dating the Orkney and Shetland Christian monuments.

There is also a link with the Pictish kingdom in the symbol on the carved bone from the Broch of Burrian (Orkney), found with an ogam-inscribed cross-shaft. The fact of finding these relics in a broch of pre-Norse days is not conclusive as to their date, for the Norse sometimes occupied brochs; that of Mousa was inhabited by a runaway couple from Norway about the year 900, and in 1155 Erlend and Maddadh's widow held it against her son, jarl Harald of Orkney. But it shows that in Christianising the northern isles other influences were at work than those of the Columban Hebrides, as one might conclude from the protracted occupation of a great part of north-eastern Scotland by the Norse. We find a few relics of their presence in the hogbacks at Inchcolm (Fife) and Brechin, and

less certainly in the ship in the Factor's Cave at
Wemyss (see Mr. J. Patrick's article in *The Reliquary*,
Jan. 1906), and in monuments commonly called
Danish, such as "Sueno's Pillar," at Forres. In this
Mr. Romilly Allen found an arrangement of knots
characteristically Scandinavian, as at Aspatria (Cumberland), Braddan (I. o. M.) and Clonmacnois ; otherwise this elaborate shaft is unlike Norse, but like
Pictish work ; it is one of those monuments in which
two influences meet, and it may help towards the true
dating of the mysterious Pictish style if this stone
proves to be of the Viking Age.   At Forres we are on
the border of country long held by the Norse ; Burg-
head was a Viking stronghold, and there we find a
"hart and hound" stone in their style (No. 7, in Mr.
Romilly Allen's *Early Christian Monuments of Scotland ;* No. 11 also might be Viking work).   Going
north we reach the Scandinavian relics of Caithness ;
the rune-inscribed "Ingulf" cross at Thurso is
comparatively late.

Leaving out, therefore, ogam stones without ornament and difficult to date, we have a series of
Orkney and Shetland monuments, some bearing
ogams, which fall into line with Manx and Scottish
work of the late tenth· to the twelfth centuries.
The conclusion seems to be that the age of
sculpture in Orkney and Shetland was rather after
than before the year 1000 ; that most of the relics
are those of re-introduced Christianity.   It may be
that the faith lingered, but it was not dominant
before Olaf Tryggvason forcibly converted jarl Sigurd

(p. 250) or about 1000. Not until half a century later was there a bishop, Henry (see *Orkney and Shet-land Old Lore*, Jan. 1907, *Diplomatarium*, p. 1), appointed by the see of York, followed by Thorolf, appointed 1056 by the archbishop of Bremen. Christ's Kirk, in Birsay, the first church known to have been built by the Norse, dates from a little after 1050, though Dietrichson and Meyer (*Monu-menta Orcadica*, Christiania, 1906) think that there may have been a somewhat earlier St. Olaf's church in Kirkwall, and three tiny Norse chapels on Sanday dating from the heathen time, but later than the Pictish period because they are built with mortar. St. Magnus' church at Egilsey, dated by Dr. Anderson about 1000, is thought by Dietrichson and Meyer to be not earlier than 1135, though an earlier church existed on the spot.

The same authors find remains to illustrate every period of Orkney history. At Toftsness on Sanday, the nearest point to Norway, seems to have been the first Norse settlement, a populous place on the site of a previous Celtic village, and defended by a stone rampart resembling pre-historic fortifications in Norway. This is still called Coligarth, in 1693 written Cuningsgar, and obviously meaning "the king's garth." At Tranaby are interments of the heathen age known as "the Bloody Tuacks," and Ivar's Knowe on Sanday may be the grave of Ivar, son of jarl Ragnvald of Mœri, killed in the expe-dition which brought the islands under the power of Harald Fairhair. As weregild for his son, Harald

gave Orkney to Ragnvald, who made over the jarldom
to his brother Sigurd. He joined Thorstein the Red
in the conquest of all northern Scotland, and died
after his fight with Maelbrigd of the Tusk. The
identification of Thorstein with the Oistin of Irish
annals has led to the placing of these events fifteen
or twenty years too early; if we date the death of
Sigurd 872 (as usually fixed) we are forced to allow
the next important jarl, Torf-Einar, a reign of sixty
years, and to place the invasion of Harald Fairhair
just before, rather than just after, the visit of bishop
Eardwulf to Whithorn, which seems improbable: we
also get too little time for the development of Olaf
the White's kingdom, and the conquests of Thorstein
the Red. But if we understand "Oistin" as Eystein,
(see p. 225), and place the invasion of Harald
about 880, and the death of Sigurd about 888, the
chronology of the whole period becomes possible.
Dr. J. Anderson identified "Cyder Hall" on the
Oykel with the Siwardhoch of 1224, and the Ekkjal
of the Saga as the scene of Jarl Sigurd's death and
burial.

Einar, son of jarl Ragnvald, may have come to the
Orkneys about 890, and he died 936. He is said to
have taught the Orkneymen the use of peat as fuel,
whence his name Torf-Einar; there are traditions that
the islands were covered with coppice before the
coming of the Norse, and, as in Iceland, the earlier
generations were doubtless improvident in their use of
wood. But the knowledge of peat seems to have
been derived from Ireland rather than from Norway.

Einar's name is also connected with an important social revolution. He revenged his father by slaying Harald Fairhair's son, Halfdan Hálegg; Dietrichson thinks that the scene of the revenge was at Tresness on Sanday, where a cairn may be Halfdan's grave. The "blood-eagle" by which he was executed was rather a form of ignominious sacrifice to Odin than an ingenious variety of torture; and it called for vengeance on Harald's part. He fined the Orkneys sixty marks of gold, which Einar paid on condition that the landowners gave up their odal rights to him.

Of his three sons, Arnkel and Erlend fell with Eirík Bloodaxe at Stainmoor (954?), and the survivor, Thorfinn Hausakljúf (Skull-cleaver), by his marriage with Grelaug, daughter of Dungal, Donnchadh or Duncan of Duncans-bæ, added Caithness to Orkney. He was buried at Haugseid (Hoxa, South Ronaldsay), and Dietrichson, quoting a tradition given by Low in 1774, thinks that his grave may be seen in a mound formed out of the ruins of a broch.

About this time, if there is any germ of truth in a legend to be found in the later and partly fictitious *Fljótsdæla-saga*, Shetland was ruled by a jarl named Björgúlf, connected by marriage with Denmark; but this statement is not confirmed.

Eirík Bloodaxe left an evil legacy to the islands in his daughter Ragnhild, who married and murdered three of Thorfinn's sons one after another. At Howardsty (Hávardsteigr), near the famous stones of Stennis, the largest of a group of Norse barrows was found to contain an urn with ashes, conjectured to be the remains

of Hávard, the second of the brothers. The last,
Hlödver, married Edna (Eithne), daughter of King
Cearbhall of Ireland, and their son was Jarl Sigurd,
who, in order to gain the help of the Orkneymen
against the Scots of the mainland, restored the odal
rights which Torf-Einar had taken from them. The
restoration was probably incomplete ; we find later a
further restitution, and at this time perhaps the rights
were given only to each owner personally, and for his
lifetime. But.Sigurd was successful in his conquests
on the mainland. He married the daughter of King
Malcolm of Scotland, and fell at the battle of Clontarf in 1014. In this battle he fought on the side of
the heathen against the Christians, though, according
to a saga-story, King Olaf Tryggvason in 997 had
visited Orkney, and forcibly converted the jarl and
his men. But about this time Christianity, though
not unknown earlier, and not fully adopted until later,
was becoming recognised among the Northmen of all
countries.

Sigurd's son Thorfinn, succeeding at the age of
five to Caithness, ultimately made himself master of
Orkney and Shetland, as well as of all the Norse
colonies in Scotland, including Galloway. His brother
Brusi, with whom he had divided Orkney at the
command of King Olaf the Saint, died in 1031,
leaving a son Ragnvald. Surviving the battle of
Stiklestad, where he had fought by the side of Olaf,
and campaigns in Russia, where he followed Harald
Hardrádi, Ragnvald returned to Orkney with a commission from King Magnus Olafsson to hold two-thirds

of the jarldom. For eight years there was peace
between the two jarls ; after the sea-fight off Rauda-
björg (1045) Ragnvald fled to Norway, and returning
burnt Thorfinn's house at Orphir. Ragnvald himself
lived at Kirkwall (Kirkju-vágr), where he perhaps
founded the town which, Dietrichson remarks, is laid
out on the plan of old Norse towns. At Birsay Thorfinn's wooden hall was no doubt on the site of the
later stone structure, which again was replaced by
Robert Stuart's palace, built in the sixteenth century.
Thorfinn's escape from the burning hall at Orphir,
with his wife Ingibjörg in his arms, and his voyage to
Caithness, is one of the most picturesque episodes of
the *Orkneyinga-saga*, full as it is of picturesque detail.
After the death of Ragnvald he was recognised by
Harald Hardrádi ; made a pilgrimage to Rome,
founded the bishopric of Orkney, and died in 1064.

His sons Paul and Erlend accompanied Harald
Hardrádi on the invasion which ended at Stamford
Bridge. In their time, according to Dietrichson, St.
Peter's at Birsay and a church at Deerness, now
destroyed, were built in stone, imitating the plan and
detail of old Norse wooden churches. Hákon, the
son of Paul, induced King Magnus Barefoot to invade
Orkney for the furtherance of his personal interests ;
but Magnus deposed Paul and Erlend, who shortly
died in Norway, and he placed his own son Sigurd
over Orkney (1098). When Sigurd became king of
Norway (1103), Hákon and his cousin Magnus
Erlendsson held the jarldom jointly. Dissension
broke out : they met for battle at Thingwold in

Rendall, the Thingstead of the islands, but were
parted; they met again at Egilsey, where Dietrichson
thinks an old Celtic church was the one mentioned
in the saga, and Magnus was put to death (Easter,
April 16, 1115). Hákon in penitence made pilgrimage to Rome and Palestine, and returning ruled in
peace. Magnus became regarded as a martyr and a
saint.

The two sons of Hákon reigned after his death
(1122 or 1123)—Harald "the smooth-spoken," and
Paul "the silent." Harald lived at Orfjara (Orphir),
where still can be seen the ruins of the round church,
built, like others of the twelfth century, in imitation of
the church of the Holy Sepulchre. It may have been
erected by his father after returning from Jerusalem,
1118, but Orphir is not mentioned as Hákon's resi-
dence, though it was the home of his sons, and the
first mention of the church is in 1136, in connexion
with the hall. The foundations of this hall, "the
Earl's Bu at Orphir," have been discovered recently,
and described by Mr. A. W. Johnston (*Proc. S. A.
Scot.*, xxxvii., and *Saga-book of the Viking Club*). Jarl
Harald is said to have been killed by a poisoned
shirt intended for his brother, and then Paul reigned
until Kali Kolsson, who took the name of Ragnvald,
the nephew of St. Magnus, came from Norway and
seized half the Orkneys. Paul was captured by Svein
Asleifarson, a Viking chief who lived in a castle (now
destroyed) on Damsey; Swendro chapel at Westness
is supposed to commemorate the capture; and Paul
was done to death in Athol, the ruler of which,

Maddadh, had married his sister. Harald, the son of Maddadh, became jarl of Orkney, sharing the power with Ragnvald.

In the winter of 1152–53 Ragnvald and a party of Norse under Erling Skakki came to the Orkney main-land on their way to the East. Some of these cru-saders broke open the Maeshowe, as one of the runic inscriptions declares (see Dietrichson and Meyer's *Monumenta Orcadica*, pp. 30 and 110–115). Most of these scribbles merely give the name of the visitor; some add that of his lady-love; a few have special interest. Nos. 19 and 20 tell us what the vikings thought of this prehistoric chambered mound :— "This mound was raised before Lodbrok's; his sons, they were clever; there were scarcely any other such men as they were. The Jorsalfarers (crusaders) broke open the Orkahaug (*i.e.* Maeshowe, which appears to be a later name). . . . It was long ago that much treasure was hidden here. . . . Happy is he who can find the great treasure." Nos. 16 and 18 are written in "twig-runes" which have been explained by Magnus Olsen as forming a verse :—

> These runes the man wrote
> Who is most rune-skilled west over sea,
> With that axe which Gauk owned,—
> Trandil's son from the south country.

No. 22 in similar cryptic runes gives the name of the carver as Tryg (Trandil's son).

While jarl Ragnvald was on his journey to Jeru-salem a new claimant appeared in Erlend, son of Harald of the poisoned shirt. He carried off

Margaret, widow of Maddadh and Harald's mother, to
the broch of Mousa, and not only defended it against
the young jarl, but, with the support of King Eystein
of Norway and Svein Asleifarson the viking, made
good his claim to the greater part of Orkney and
Caithness. When Ragnvald returned there were
three jarls, who met in battle at Knarrarstad (Knar-
stoun) in 1156. Erlend, however, did not long survive,
and Ragnvald fell at Kalfadal (Calder, in Caithness)
shortly afterwards. His father Kol and he had founded
(about 1137) and partly built the cathedral of St.
Magnus at Kirkwall, completing the choir, according
to Dietrichson and Meyer, before 1153. To provide
money for the building Ragnvald restored full odal
rights to the Orkneymen, and as jarl Sigurd had
already made a similar restitution, it is thought that on
the first occasion the rights were restored only for the
owner's lifetime, while Ragnvald granted them in
perpetuity. By his " pilgrimage " and church-build-
ing this poet-jarl, no saintly person, died in odour of
sanctity, and was canonised in 1192.

At his death, about 1158, the Cistercian abbey on
Eyin helga (Enhallow) may have been already founded,
and during this period Kolbein Hruga built his small
stone keep on the island of Weir, where "Cobbie
Row," according to tradition, used until modern
times to haunt the ruins. His son was Bjarni, bishop
of Orkney 1188–1223, who continued the building of
the cathedral, and according to Dr. Jón Stefánsson
(*Orkney and Shetland Old Lore*, April 1907) wrote the
Jarla-sögur, which we know as *Orkneyinga-saga*.

Jarl Harald Maddadh's son, having got rid of rivals, spent the rest of his long reign in making enemies. By his second marriage with Gormflaith, daughter of Malcolm MacEth (the adventurer Vémund, once a monk of Furness), he became enemy of King William the Lion, and lost a great part of Caithness ; by his partisanship in Norse affairs he became enemy of King Sverrir and lost Shetland ; and by the outrage upon bishop John, who was blinded at Scarabolstad (Scrabster in Caithness), he made the Church his enemy. He died in 1206, aged 73. Shetland remained the immediate property of the Norse crown until it was granted to St. Clair in 1379. The outrage upon one bishop led to the extortions and the murder of the next, bishop Adam ; and jarl Harald's surviving son, John, was killed in 1231, ending the Norse line which had ruled Orkney for 350 years.

In 1232 king Alexander II. of Scotland granted Northern Caithness to Magnus, son of Gilbride, earl of Angus, and perhaps of a daughter of Harald, son of Maddadh. The king of Norway granted Magnus the jarldom of Orkney also ; and thus a portion of the old realm was placed under a ruler of Norse name and probably Norse descent, but governing the two parts of his country under two different kingdoms. His grandson Magnus accompanied King Hákon Hákonarson to the battle of Largs in 1263. John, the grandson of this Magnus, was one of those who signed the petition that the son of Edward I. should marry Margaret the Maid of Norway, who died (1290) on her way to England, at Margaret's Hope (hóp).

John's son Magnus ended the Angus line, though it is possible that his sister had married Malise, the earl of Stratherne, who founded the next dynasty. The Stratherne family was followed by the St. Clairs (1379–1469), of whom William, the last who ruled Orkney under the Norse crown, was invested by King Erik the Pomeranian, in 1434.

On the marriage between James III. of Scotland and Margaret of Denmark, her father, Christian I. of Denmark and Norway, undertook to give a dowry of 60,000 Rhine florins, 10,000 of which were to be paid in cash, and Orkney was pledged for the remainder. Only 2,000 florins, however, were paid, and King Christian made up the balance by pledging Shetland. Thus the old possessions of Norway came to the crown of Scotland, but only, in the first instance, as a pledge to be redeemed ; and it is a question which has been much discussed—whether the mortgage was foreclosed, and, if so, when ?   Mr. Gilbert Goudie, in his *Antiquities of Shetland*, states the case at some length ; we can give but the barest outline of his argument.

The continuator of Boece (Ferrerius, Paris, 1574) says that the right of redemption was renounced on the birth of a grandson (James IV.) to the Danish king, and subsequent Scottish historians repeat the story.   Torfæus, however (book iii., chapter on the subject), and other Danish historians state that re-peated efforts were made to regain the islands by offering payments of the sum due, and that a series of embassies (1549–1660) were sent to Scotland with that object. Though the Register of the Privy Council of Scotland does not record, for instance, an embassy for this purpose in 1585, the Calendar of English State Papers and various Scottish memoirs refer to it. In 1589 James VI. married the princess Anne of Denmark, and the matter was deferred during the minority of Christian IV. When he came of age James prevailed on him to allow it to stand over during their reigns. In 1640 payment was again tendered, but the troubles of the time hindered settlement. In 1660 Charles II. was approached, but managed to evade a settlement, and at the treaty of Breda (1667) the question was still left open. In the middle of the eighteenth century Frederick V. once more demanded the restitution of the islands, but in vain. Mr. Goudie, writing before the foundation of the modern Norwegian kingdom, thought that Denmark rather than Norway would have the right still to redeem, because when the two countries were disjoined in 1814 Denmark retained all the islands of the North Sea, which would include the reversion of Orkney and Shetland.

The question as it now stands is purely academical, but it was not so in the first centuries after the impignoration. The people of Orkney and Shetland were still Norse, and looked to Norway as their mother-country. In Mr. Goudie's words: "They continued to advocate causes, not to the courts of law in Scotland, but to the courts with which they were more familiar in Norway; and the native system of law and justice, of udal succession and udal tenure in land, survived in some measure, though determined efforts

R

were made at repression for at least a couple of hundred years later." In *Orkney and Shetland Old Lore*, for October 1907, is printed a series of documents, conveyances, agreements, charters, etc., ranging from 1422 to 1575, many of them in Norse, and all showing the close connexion of the islanders with Norway. For example, in 1538 the Norse king at Bergen confirms a doom of the Shetland Lawting, and describes the trial in which Gervald Williamsson won his heritage from Magnus Olsson as according to Gulathing's law. Many of the deeds relate to settlements between islanders and their relatives living in Norway. The law-terms are chiefly Norse, as :—
"athmen " = *eiðmenn* (oathmen), "arvis skopft " = *arfskipti* (division of inheritance), "oumbotht" = *umboð* (commission), "schonit" = *sjaund* (seventh day after the death, when the division of goods was made), "mensvering " = *meinsværi* (perjury, whence " manswearing "), " samengna man " = *sameignar maðr* (joint possessor), "granttis with hand and handband " = *handaband* (joining hands), "ofhintit " from *aflenda* (to hand over), "teind penny and ferde penny" = *tiundargjöf ok fjörðungsgjöf* (for in Norse law one could dispose of only one-tenth of one's patrimony and one-fourth of personally acquired goods without the consent of one's heirs).

Ecclesiastically also the islands remained Norse ; in 1491 king John of Denmark and Norway granted, in one of these documents, to Sir David Sinclair the rents and rights of the Crown over the servants of the Church in Orkney. The people's names

were Norse with few exceptions; the parishioners
of Cunningsburgh in 1576 were named Olaw (4),
Magnus (7), Ercik, Swaine, Symone (Sæmund),
Brownie (Brúnn), with Nichole, Erasmus and John,
more recent names than the heathen age but still
Norse, and the Celtic Hector; all their holdings were,
as they still remain, named in Norse. Indeed it is
hardly profitable to attempt here any survey of Orkney
and Shetland place-names; ·they are, of course, so
completely Scandinavian as to need a special volume
for their elucidation (see Dr. Jakob Jakobsen, *Dialect
and Place-names of Shetland*, 1897; and *Shetlandsöernes
Stednavne*, 1901).

George Buchanan in 1582 said that the Shetland
measures, numbers and weights were "Germanic" or
"almost old Gothic." Brand in 1701 remarked that
Shetlanders spoke Norse, though Dutch was understood
owing to the trade with Holland. In 1711 Sir Robert
Sibbald called their language "Norn" (*Norræna*), and
so late as 1770 the Rev. George Low collected the
remains of the language as then remembered on Foula,
the westernmost of the Shetlands. The ballad of
"Hildina" (trans. W. G. Collingwood, *Ork. and Shet.
Old Lore*, Ap. 1908) has been edited in a masterly
treatise, *Hildinakvædet*, by Prof. Marius Hægstad (1900),
in which the difficulties of a text dictated to one who
was entirely ignorant of the language have been cleared
up, and the "Norn" is shown to be fairly pure Norse,
with a very slight sprinkling of Danish, Færoese, Fri-
sian and English words. It may be remarked that
initial H is sometimes dropped or added; consonants

are occasionally lost; phonetic changes like those
in Icelandic and Færoese are *dn* for *rn*, *dl* and
dn for *ll* and *nn* ("kidn" for *kinn*, cheek; "godle"
for *gull*, gold; "ednin" for *örnin*, the eagle); but
the language differs from the Hebridean, not only
in the absence of Gaelic, but also in the use of
Scandinavian words other than those found in the
Western Islands, as "gronge" (*grunningr*) and not
"torsk" for a cod. Low collected also the well-
known Shetland rhyme, which Hægstad reads—

> Myrk in e liora, Luce (=ljóss) in e liunga,
> Timin e guestin e geungna.
>
> When it's mirk in the chimney it's light on the ling,
> It's the time for the guest to be journeying.

He gave also the Foula "Paternoster," which may
be compared with the old Orkney form given by
Wallace (English loan-words italicised) :—

Shetland	*Orkney*
Fy vor o er i chimeri,	Fa vor i ir i chimeri,
Halaght vara nam dit,	Helleu[r] ir i nam thite,
La konungdum din cumma,	Gilla (=Gud lat) cosdum
	(? congdum) thite cumma,
La vill din vera guerde	Veya thine mota varg gort
i vrildin sen (=som) da er	o yurn sinna gort
i chimeri (=Himmerike),	i chimeri,
Gav vus dagh u dagloght brau,	Ga vus da on da dalight
	brow vora,
Forgive sindor wara sin vi	*Firgive* vus sinna vora sin vee
forgiva gem ao sinda *gainst*	*firgive* sindara mutha vus,
wus,	
Lia wus ekè o vera *tempa*,	Lyv vus ye i *tumtation*,
but delivra wus fro adlu idlu,	min *delivra* vus fro olt ilt,
For doi ir konungdum,	
u *puri*, u *glori*, Amen.	Amen.

More than a hundred years later than Low's time

considerable relics of Norse language and folklore have been recognised in the islands.[1] One curious survival is the sea-language (noticed by the late Karl Blind, in *Saga-book of the Viking Club*, i., p. 163) by which, for example, *at sea* a church is called a " bell-house," the sea is named as " holy toyt," and a cat is spoken of as " footie," " snistal," or " vanega." Perhaps we need not accept Dr. Blind's suggestion that the last word means *Vanadis* and relates to Freyja ; nor is it quite certain that the rhyme he collected—" Nine days he hang fra de rütless tree," etc.—is a survival, through nearly 1000 years, of the famous lines of *Hávamál* about Odin's self-sacrifice.

But of all Britain, Orkney and Shetland are the most completely Scandinavian parts, and the story of the suppression of Norse life under Scottish rule is still remembered as an ancient grievance :—" The sub-version of the native laws, the imposition of the feudal system upon the odalism of the north, the appropriation of the greater part of the land by ad-venturers from Scotland—in short, the ruin of the native race " (Gilbert Goudie, *Antiquities of Shetland*, p. 214). The old system in Shetland was that of government under Fouds, Lawrightmen and Ranselmen. The Great Foud (*Fógeti*) was the chief civil official, appointed by the Crown, with a Lawman elected by the Thing at Tingwall as legal adviser and judge of assize. Parish Fouds were appointed by the

[1] See Dr. Jakob Jakobsen's elaborate dictionary of the Norse language of Shetland (Copenhagen, V. Prior ; part I., 1908).

Great Foud, to receive rents and duties in butter, oil and wadmell, and to hold Shuynd Courts for the division of estates among heirs of the deceased (see the word *sjaund*, p. 258). They were assisted by Councillors (Raadmen), but all householders were required to attend the Thing. Lawrightmen (Lögrétta-menn) were chosen by the Vardthing, and charged with the custody and application of the standards of weight and measure (cuttell, bismar and can) by which dues were paid, and with the general interests of the parish, especially at the Lawthing, when the Lawrightman was the assessor of the Foud, acting in the interests of the people. The conversion of payments from kind to coin did away with his duties. "Skathald" Mr. Goudie considers as common pasture-land for which *skat* was paid; Mr. A. W. Johnston says that it formerly meant the township, including *hagi* or pasture. Ranselmen (from *ransel*, to search a house for stolen goods, apparently equivalent to the Icelandic *rannsaka*, whence our "ransack") were appointed to inquire into cases of theft, scandal, dispute, misbehaviour, absence from church, trespass, dilapidation, vagrancy, witchcraft and contravention of laws about sheep and sheep-dogs. They came to be practically analogous to the old parish constable, and appointments were made down to 1836, and in Fair Isle even so late as 1869.

A few survivals of old Norse life may be noticed. The horizontal watermill was not a turbine, but an ordinary wheel, placed with axis vertical, and driven by a jet running through a trough and acting on one side of the wheel only : the upper millstone revolved on the spindle of the waterwheel. Some terms relating to its structure are Norse; the sile (*sigle*), or iron crossbar of the axle which turned the wheel; the grütte (*grötte*), or nave of the lower millstone, through which the spindle passed ; and the ludr, or loft of the little house in which the mill worked; (for a full description see Mr. Goudie, *op. cit.*, pp. 246–281). Mills of this kind were used in Sweden and Norway (but not found in Denmark), the Færoes, Orkney and Shetland, Caithness and Sutherland, the Hebrides, the Isle of Man, and in parts of Ireland, where they were called " Danish mills." They are known in other parts of the world, but their frequency in these Norse countries suggests a common origin dating from the Viking Age. The kollie (*kola*, in Scottish " crusie "), an oil lamp with a double shell ; the bismar (*bismari*), a steelyard weighing machine ; the tuskar (*torfskeri*), a peat spade, all keep their old names ; but the old customs survived in the short scythe with its long handle, the one-stilted wooden plough, and the rivling, or shoes of raw hide formerly common to all northern lands.

A not uninteresting sidelight is thrown upon the relations of Northumbria after the Conquest with Scandinavian Caithness and Galloway in the story of King William the Wanderer. It is told in Norman French of the twelfth century by two different poets, one of whom seems to have been Chrestien de Troyes (printed by Francisque Michel in *Chroniques Anglo-Normands*, 1840, and Englished by W. G. Collingwood,

1904). It relates the adventures of an imaginary king
of England whose wife was carried off by Vikings to
a Scottish seaport, his children to the Norse colony
of Caithness, where they were fostered by kindly fur-
traders, and he himself, after long wanderings, is brought
to the service of a merchant in Galinde (Galuide) or
Gavaide (Galvaide), that is to say, Galloway. The
story, like others of the period, is of British origin,
and can have been composed only in Cumbria or
Northumbria towards the end of the eleventh century,
and among people who, though they had a horror of
the piracy of an age by then passing away, were in
close connexion with Norse trading colonies in
Scotland. The great jarl is sketched with admiration,
perhaps from the famous Thorfinn ; the kind Caithness
traders are drawn to the life, not without hints of their
homeliness as compared with the refinement of the
South, and the benevolent and wealthy shipowner of
Galloway is the true ancestor of the merchant princes
who have made British commerce and philanthropy
famous. The unconscious testimony of this contemporary picture of manners and men tells us, like
the monuments, a tale untold by the curt annals of
bloodshed and rapine, now no longer to be regarded
as the whole history of Scandinavian Britain.

INDEX

265